PRAISE FOR
FEAR DYNAMICS

"*Fear Dynamics* is the remarkable story of Stephen J. Dietrich overcoming a challenging upbringing to achieve *both* the pinnacle of professional success and personal fulfillment and happiness. Stephen offers techniques he developed on his journey that are applicable to everyone. His story teaches us that life isn't all about accomplishments—it's about relationships. Bottom line: *Fear Dynamics* can help you tackle the fear and anxiety in your life to be in control of the person you want to be."

—John Elway, NFL Hall of Fame quarterback, two-time Super Bowl champion

"*Fear Dynamics* is an incredible story of transformation, and it doesn't stop at the why—it gives you the how. If you keep falling back into the same bad habits, the techniques in this book will help you break that pattern for good."

—Mel Robbins, *New York Times* bestselling author and host of the award-winning *Mel Robbins Podcast*

"Stephen J. Dietrich takes the reader on a brave and vulnerable journey through trauma and adversity to acceptance and empowerment, with lessons and tools that are very much shared and needed in our conversations and communities today. Trauma and adversity are incredibly common, but so too is healing when we share our stories, our struggles, our triumphs, and our resilience. This topic, and the tools he shares, are integral to transformational and sustainable change to help and to heal."

—**Dr. Kate Tumelty Felice,** professor of education, psychology, and integrative health; a national educator and subject matter expert on adversity, trauma, and resilience

"Stephen J. Dietrich has taken his challenging start in life and harnessed lessons for all of us. What might have stopped many in their tracks is the bedrock for Stephen's growth. He draws us in with his struggle, pauses, and gives us tools and strategies to capture our own fear to use as a strength. He's mastered these skills for personal and professional development . . . and since the law is a people business, that's a recipe for meaningful achievement all around."

—**William Shepherd,** former statewide prosecutor of Florida, chair of the American Bar Criminal Justice Section, and current BigLaw partner

"The fears that so many of us face, whether childhood trauma, debilitating setbacks, or overwhelming anxiety, can be calmed with confidence. In authentically sharing his own path, Stephen J. Dietrich offers a powerful resilience that is available to anybody. Instead of telling us to just suck it up, Dietrich reminds us how we too can show ourselves compassion and write our own story."

—Merril Hoge, inspirational speaker, author, former ESPN analyst and NFL running back

"Fear Dynamics is an *amazing* story of a best-in-class M&A attorney who navigated disastrous parental experiences and survived, thrived, and excelled in life. Stephen J. Dietrich tells his story, and more importantly shares invaluable tools that can help everyone, regardless of their life journey, to improve their relationships and lives."

—Michael Maroone, chairman and CEO, Maroone USA

www.amplifypublishinggroup.com

Fear Dynamics: Harnessing Fear and Anxiety to Create Lasting
Happiness and Meaningful Achievement

For more information, please contact:
Amplify Publishing, an imprint of Amplify Publishing Group
620 Herndon Parkway, Suite 220
Herndon, VA 20170
info@amplifypublishing.com

Library of Congress Control Number: 2024902847

CPSIA Code: PRV0424A

ISBN-13: 978-1-63755-973-4

Printed in the United States

To Nicholas. Without knowing it, you motivated my transformation each day as I started my journey, because I had to be a better father for you. In the end, I became a better person for me as well.

FEAR
DYNAMICS

Harnessing fear and anxiety
to create *lasting happiness*
and *meaningful achievement*

STEPHEN J. DIETRICH, JD

amplify
an imprint of Amplify Publishing Group

Contents

Introduction 1

1 A Perfect Family on the Outside   9

Fear Dynamics Technique #1
Accept Yourself and Your Past 14

2 Dad, the Molester   21

Fear Dynamics Technique #2
Checking in with Your Inner Little Guy or Gal 31

Fear Dynamics Technique #3
Make Eye Contact 40

Fear Dynamics Technique #4
Build in a Pause 48

3 Mom, the Alcoholic   61

Fear Dynamics Technique #5
Create a Decision Tree 71

4 Life Goes On   83

5 Meeting Mrs. Right When I Was Mr. Wrong   91

Fear Dynamics Technique #6
Get Off Autopilot 101

6   *The Crash and Burn*   111

Fear Dynamics Technique #7
Stop Compartmentalizing 119

7   *Saving My Family, Saving Myself*   129

Fear Dynamics Technique #8
Don't Be a Duck 137

8   *Fear Dynamics at Work and at Home*   147

Fear Dynamics Technique #9
Tackling Fear Dynamics at Home and at Work
with Rational Decision-Making 161

9   *Balance Fear and Trust*   179

Fear Dynamics Technique #10
Making Big Changes with Tiny Habits 186

Fear Dynamics Technique #11
Train Your Brain 190

10   *Memories and the Future*   209

Acknowledgments 221

About the Author 223

Introduction

"It looks to me like you turned out okay. So, what's your problem?" This is what my dad asked me when I finally confronted him face-to-face about the years of sexual abuse I endured at his hands—apparently unbeknownst to my mentally-distant and emotionally-neglectful alcoholic mother.

Granted, I did *appear* as though I had turned out okay. I was a well-pedigreed attorney, married, and making a good living. But as we all know, looks can be deceiving. Behind the facade I was a mess—riddled with anxiety, closed off emotionally, and completely unable to enjoy any of my objective success.

In my youth, I developed ways to conceal my family's abnormalities and abuse. I learned to cope with my shame that accompanied them. I mastered avoidance, suppressed my desires, and kept my opinions to myself. I numbed myself to the pain, hid any vulnerabilities, and covered for my parents' shortcomings. I built a mental fortress to protect my emotional self from the slings and arrows of child abuse and neglect. Detachment was better than the alternative—actually experiencing the pain of being neglected and abused by the two people in my world who were supposed to care for me and protect me.

I had no idea that these coping mechanisms I developed and perfected in my childhood would come back to harm me later in life. They worked well when I was a child in a dysfunctional and abusive home, but as I matured, they became more a hindrance than a help in maintaining relationships and achieving personal and professional fulfillment.

As a result, for nearly my entire life I drifted between relationships, avoided authentic connections with others, and lived completely disconnected from myself and my emotions. Hollow on the inside, a fraud on the outside.

Upon leaving home for college, I thought that I was leaving my past behind and that I knew the path forward to happiness and success. But I was wrong. I did not recognize in the slightest the grip that my anxiety and curated behaviors had on me. Constant anxiety permeated my existence. I had no idea how it felt not to be anxious. I thought, *This is your life.*

Only after I found my soul mate, married her, had a son together—and then nearly lost it all—did I realize that I had to change *me.* I engaged in various forms of therapy to examine and understand my past and the impact it was having on me and on my thoughts and behaviors. Throughout this process, I discovered several techniques for replacing my counterproductive thought patterns and behaviors with productive and supportive ones.

Change did not happen overnight, nor was the process smooth and linear. Progress came in fits and starts. I tried a variety of therapies and self-help programs—some more useful than others. I took small steps forward, then stumbled back. I experienced alternating periods of clarity, confusion, and despair.

As I improved, I continued making minor adjustments and practicing techniques until they became second nature. Over time, all my efforts and these small adjustments resulted in a major positive transformation.

Today, I am comfortable in my skin and I enjoy my life. I cherish my close relationships. I look others in the eye and engage in whatever is transpiring in the present. I am no longer a raw nerve overreacting to the slightest provocation. I think and act decisively, deliberately, and proactively. I know what I want, and I pursue it rationally through a careful examination of facts. I'm not perfect, but I'm perfectly happy with myself and where I am.

> I'm not perfect, but I'm perfectly
> happy with myself and where I am.

Perhaps you see yourself in this description. Maybe to everyone else you look fine on the outside, but are struggling inside. I know better than most that outward success is not necessarily indicative of internal happiness and fulfillment. Conversely, maybe your struggle is external. Maybe you're dealing with difficult family matters (or members), having trouble advancing in your career, or feeling overwhelmed by financial strain.

Whether your struggle is internal, external, or both, if you're suffering from anxiety, fear, sadness, or feelings of inadequacy, burden, or bitterness, you are the reason I wrote this book.

This book is comprised of chapters focused on my personal history followed by techniques or activities that I have utilized to help me change, not just my behavior, but my actual way of processing thoughts and feelings in any situation. Who am I to be giving you advice? I'm not a licensed therapist or a researcher with a PhD in human behavior. Instead, I am person who struggled his whole life with feeling disconnected, anxious, and vaguely unhappy.

This book is a product of what I learned on my journey from paralyzing fear and anxiety to confidence and joy. When I look back on this journey, I realize that I needed to put as much work into achieving happiness and fulfillment as I did into reaching any other goal. My life was a chaotic mess, and I needed to find a way to order it and learn to enjoy my life.

Remember, you don't have to hit rock bottom to start improving your life and leading a satisfying day-to-day existence, but you do have to put intentional and genuine effort into creating a rewarding, happy life. My hope is that this book frees you from fear and anxiety and enables you to discover who you truly are, achieve your dreams, and experience a deeper level of happiness and self-fulfillment.

While I was working on myself and using these techniques to improve my personal and professional relationships and out-comes, I got to thinking not only about how my fears impact my relationships, but how the interaction of the fears and anxieties of others also impacts relationships between two or more people. As they say, "It takes two to tango."

Individual fears and anxieties of all people in a situation influ-ence the give and take of the relationship. I decided to call this interplay "fear dynamics." Once I named this phenomenon in my own life, I saw fear dynamics everywhere: At work, when a colleague avoided responding to a client because he was afraid of the client's response, which only served to create a larger and more unproductive client reply; At home, when my son would stomp out of the room after my wife asked him to practice piano because he had a recital coming up.

Both my wife and my son were afraid and nervous about the upcoming performance and their fears interacted with each other to heighten the situation. When I realized the power that fear—and the resulting anxiety—has in our relationship with ourselves and with others, it led me to be able to manage the anxiety and engage more calmly and clearly in all my relationships, professional and personal.

Introducing Fear Dynamics

Specifically, I define fear dynamics as the behavior and communication patterns that occur during interpersonal interactions in which one or more of the people involved are consciously or unconsciously reacting to fears. The fear in fear dynamics is the same feeling evoked in any frightening situation, but dynamics come into play only when other people are affected by the fear. In other words, fear dynamics has a relational aspect to it.

Fear dynamics significantly impacts personal and business interactions, as well as social interactions. For example, imagine you are afraid of offending your friends by declining invitations to events that for whatever reason make you uncomfortable. The fear you feel might prevent you from expressing your authentic preferences and establishing boundaries. As a result, you might end up attending events you dislike. All the while, your friends remain unaware of your discomfort. This scenario illustrate how fear dynamics can strain personal relationships and hinder honest communication.

In a business setting, if you are afraid to share ideas with colleagues outside of your immediate division because a supervisor perceives such interactions as a threat, the fear is negatively affecting your ability to communicate and innovate with colleagues. The result is harm to the organization overall.

In these pages, I share my story and offer advice on what worked to help me think more clearly, feel less fearful and anxious on a minute-by-minute basis, and live a happier and more satisfying life. The book is organized with narrative chapters followed by a Fear Dynamics-related technique to help you harness your own fears and anxieties.

> *In these pages, I share my story and offer advice on what worked to help me think more clearly, feel less fearful and anxious on a minute-by-minute basis, and live a happier and more satisfying life.*

It's customary in books like these to include an author disclaimer and it's appropriate for me to do so here. The advice, strategies, and tactics set forth in this book are based upon my personal experience and reflection. As I said, I am not a mental health professional, a doctor, or a scientist; I'm a lawyer. I am sharing this material to illustrate and demonstrate what I have learned and discovered, and what has worked for me. As a result, the information in this book about fear dynamics is provided for general informational purposes only and may not reflect current mental health thinking or practices. No information contained in this book should be construed as mental health advice from Stephen J. Dietrich, JD, nor is this book intended to be a substitute for mental health treatment or counsel on any subject matter. No reader of this book should act or refrain from acting on the basis of any information included in, or accessible through, this book without seeking the appropriate mental health advice on the particular facts and circumstances at issue from a licensed mental health professional in the recipient's state, country or other appropriate licensing jurisdiction.

I hope this book enables you to understand fear dynamics, achieve your personal and professional goals faster and easier and with fewer setbacks than I experienced. Think of it as a toolkit on your winding path to happiness, self-fulfillment, and a deeper connection with yourself and others.

Important Information for Readers

This book delves into the personal experiences of abuse, including emotional and sexual abuse, as experienced by the author. If you or someone you know is struggling or in need of support, please remember that you are not alone. Help is available. Below is a list of organizations dedicated to offering support, counseling, and resources to those experiencing abuse:

- National Domestic Violence Hotline: 1-800-799-SAFE (7233)
- National Sexual Assault Hotline: 1-800-656-HOPE (4673)
- Childhelp National Child Abuse Hotline: 1-800-422-4453
- The National Center for Victims of Crime: 1-202-467-8700

Please consider reaching out if you find yourself in need of support. Remember, seeking help is a sign of strength. Your safety and wellbeing are important, and these organizations are available to help.

Fear dynamics noun /ˈfir dī-ˈna-miks/

1: the behavior and communication patterns that occur during interpersonal interactions in which one or more of the people involved are consciously or unconsciously reacting to fears

Chapter 1

A PERFECT FAMILY ON THE OUTSIDE

f I had a Wikipedia page, it would tell the objective tale of Stephen J. Dietrich, the child of accomplished parents, raised in an upper-middle-class rural neighborhood. I became a successful attorney, devoted husband, and caring father. My parents were well-respected college professors working in different departments—my father in history, and my mother in psychology.

By all outward appearances I lived a charmed life. Academics and sports always came easily to me. I skated through high school, worked hard in college, and got through law school. I am now married to a wonderful woman, and we have an intelligent, thoughtful, and active son. I could have been the poster child for upper-middle-class America. I had it made. But did I?

The story you are about to read tells a much different tale when you dig beneath the surface.

Meet My Family

I grew up in the Midwest—north central Wisconsin more specifically, and, even more precisely, in a small town called Plover, just outside of Stevens Point. Stevens Point is reputed to have the greatest number of taverns in one square mile of any city in the nation. I don't know if that's true, but I can tell you the winter weather was bleak and drinking seemed to be a favorite pastime for many residents, and definitely for my parents.

I have a sister two years older than me and a brother four years younger. A little over a year before I was born, my parents had a baby girl who died when she was just a few days old. According to the family story, the doctor told my parents to have another baby as soon as possible to avoid anxiety around having another child.

My parents did as directed, but unfortunately, I don't think my mom was emotionally healed or had finished grieving the loss before I was born. Instead of showering me with love and affection, she kept her distance. Obviously, I don't have evidence of this based on my own memories and observations, but anecdotes from both of my parents indicate that during infancy I spent a significant amount of time alone in my crib.

As the family narrative goes, I barely said a word until I was three years old. It was as if I were waiting until I could say exactly what I wanted to say because even then I was afraid of making a mistake. This dread of dire consequences over even minor mistakes pervaded my family. An air of trepidation accompanied any action or opinion in our house. I can't actually recall receiving any authentic affection or nurturing from either of my parents. Believe me, I tried.

We lived in Plover because my parents were professors at the University of Wisconsin–Stevens Point. Despite living there for twenty years, they never considered themselves to be from

Wisconsin. They saw themselves as intellectual East Coasters. They were friendly with neighbors but had few friends. I think they saw themselves as better than the people of Plover. For example, when they parked our boat near the sandbar on the Wisconsin River a few miles downriver from our house, they remained on board, rarely wading through the shallow water at the sandbar to another family's pontoon boat for idle chatter or gossip. A friendly wave to passers-by was the full extent of their involvement.

My parents didn't even talk much to each other, each taking up their respective afternoon positions, father at the back sipping a beer and mother in a lounge chair up front nursing a gin and tonic, both heads buried in a book or scholarly article. The possibility of them socializing with other families on a regular and comfortable basis was inconceivable to me.

From the Outside Looking In . . .

I do believe that neighbors and people in the community thought we were a normal, albeit aloof, family. My siblings and I were respectful, punctual, and, for the most part, friendly and articulate. We attended school regularly, earned good grades, played sports, had friends, and were always dressed appropriately in clean clothes. Outsiders probably considered us to be a little overly intellectual.

My best friend in high school would always tease me that, after every visit to our home, he needed a dictionary to look up at least one word he had heard. For the most part we appeared to be a normal family, but the truth is, we were far from normal.

My mother was a functional alcoholic for many years until she dropped the "functional" and her employer mandated she enter rehab or her tenure would be revoked (I was eighteen years old at the time and in the second quarter of my freshman year in college). When I was living at home, she was some level of drunk most weekend afternoons and nights. She exhibited two behaviors when she was drunk: semi-comatose isolation or bitter rage. My sister received more than her fair share of the vitriol, but I was on the receiving end as well.

My mom was unhappy with how her life had turned out and she had to let me know, specifically, what a personal disappointment I was to her. I remember regularly waking up at night to my mother's high decibel rants, often directed toward my father, about how she hated her life. Mornings after these nights I would hunt around the house with morbid curiosity to see what damage had been done. My most exciting discovery was a shattered bathroom mirror one winter morning.

During the weekdays my mother was so tired or worn out from the chemical abuse that she shuffled like a zombie through the house. I believe she mustered all her spirit to get through her work obligations and had little, if any, positive energy left for anyone at home.

My dad did everything. He shopped, he cooked, he cleaned. He led us to believe that our mother was completely incapable of performing her "maternal" duties. He let us know that he was the parent you could depend upon and that we needed him.

He also let us know how burdened he felt at every turn and expected us to be grateful to spend time with him. For example, every year my dad would choose a Saturday in early December to make Christmas cookies. This sounds like the makings of a wonderful holiday memory. Unfortunately, it was the Bataan Death March of cookie-making.

He would make cookie recipe after cookie recipe while directing us siblings to grease the pan, scoop the dough, whip the frosting, and decorate. There was little holiday merriment. It was an exhausting day full of grumbling from Dad. And at the end we weren't permitted to eat the cookies, except on rare, special days designated by my dad. Not one bite. These cookies were for Christmas, he would explain. On the other hand, my dad would take a plate into his home office while he graded exams or worked on a paper. Or to curry favor, he might offer a plate to a neighbor or share some with his officemates on campus.

By the time Christmas arrived, I really didn't even want a cookie—although I gobbled them up when they became available. This was emblematic of my family. It looked like a great Dietrich holiday tradition, but it was really a sham masking our dysfunction in a hastily-frosted snowman cookie.

We had all the trappings of a healthy, normal family—two parents, both gainfully employed, three apparently well-cared-for children, a nice home, a boat, neighbors, and friends. I think my mom and dad even convinced themselves they were good parents. They worked hard, provided for their children, and sent them to good schools, put in occasional appearances at school and athletic events, and so on.

We certainly appeared to be turning out okay, but even with all their education, they were blind to the emotional and psychological scars they left behind. For years, I too was unable to acknowledge the damage they had done.

FEAR DYNAMICS TECHNIQUE #1

ACCEPT YOURSELF AND YOUR PAST

I share my story of the neglect and abuse I suffered at the hands of my parents and my struggle to gain mental and emotional health not to be salacious or vengeful or to elicit sympathy. I share it because it sheds light on how I had become such a broken person.

For better or worse, my parents provided the nurture to my nature. The effects my home environment had on me defined me up to a point, but in order to develop beyond this person I had been trained to become, I needed to accept and understand my past. When I started my most intensive therapy work, I learned that insights into my past would illuminate the path to my future.

One of the first crucial tenets I learned to internalize was that I needed to accept myself for who I was at that specific point in my life. Not that it is easy, but what I learned is that self-fulfillment is possible only with self-acceptance because self-acceptance ensures that whatever changes you decide to make will align with the person you really are.

If you deny yourself and try to become something you're not, any changes you make will result in a less authentic version of you.

You will be conflicted, uncomfortable in your own skin, and you will continue to be dissatisfied and unhappy.

> *Self-fulfillment is possible only with self-acceptance.*

In many ways, self-acceptance is the antidote to neglect and abuse. It enables us to neutralize any denial and rejection we experienced in our past so we can begin to overcome the resulting low self-esteem and lack of self-confidence. By accepting ourselves we reject the way people in our past have tried to define, contain, and control us. We refuse to continue to be a victim of their denial and rejection of our true selves.

The first part of my story was written by others. I realized later in life that only I could write the rest of my story. And the rest of my story began the day I accepted myself for who I was right at that moment.

Your past and personal trauma shape your thoughts, influence your behaviors, and guide your actions, but they don't define you or prevent you from becoming the person you want to be. Deep inside is the essence of who you are, and it does not change in response to your circumstances—however terrible they may be.

Your essence is who you are and the potential of who you can become. It is the oak tree in the acorn. I believe it is of vital importance to accept yourself and your past, in its entirety, without letting the traumatic events define you or limit what you want to be, do, and have.

> *The first part of my story was written by others. I realized later in life that only I could write the rest of my story.*

I was not a person who loved therapy. I kept stopping until I finally had to dig in and work hard to understand myself or lose my family. I thought at length about my past before I was able to discuss it with therapists, and I hesitated for even longer before I was able to sit down and write the details of the neglect, abuse, and dysfunction.

The sexual abuse was the most difficult for me to come to terms with and share. I needed to be able to accept that these traumatic events happened to me in order for me to be able to heal. For years I tried to deny that I was damaged. I achieved my external success through sheer effort and determination, but I was broken inside.

I had to accept and understand myself and how I had become so broken. Only then could I begin to reverse the damage, heal, and begin to form authentic and lasting connections with others.

> *I had to accept and understand myself and how I had become so broken. Only then could I begin to reverse the damage, heal, and begin to form authentic and lasting connections with others.*

As part of this Fear Dynamics Technique, I encourage you to look at your past, at the people, events, and experiences that shaped your worldview, the way you think, and your behaviors, and accept all of it as part of your story. Then, examine it closely to gain an understanding of how you became the person you are now. You may recognize events in your past during which you acted in ways you now regret or make you feel ashamed. I encourage you to accept those parts, too.

Your power to change is in direct proportion to your ability to genuinely accept yourself and your past. Only then can you begin to undo the damage and develop into the person you have the potential to become.

Glean Insight from Your Past

To be clear, I am not advocating a victim mentality. Your past is not an excuse, but an explanation. Avoid the common temptation to use past experiences to excuse mistakes or weaknesses. Instead, use past experiences as a beacon to help you see and understand yourself and the reasons you may think and act in certain ways in your current life.

I grappled with having a very low sense of self-worth due to my experiences growing up. Accepting this fact helped me understand why my initial reactions to comments or situations were always through the lens of low self-esteem. I was able to develop tools to filter my reactions, think objectively and help me to make authentic connections with people. I will always struggle with anxiety issues and have moments of self-doubt, but now I have Fear Dynamics Techniques to more effectively manage my thoughts and feelings. I control them; they do not control me.

When my son was young, I—like many parents—read parenting books. I noticed that the theme of acceptance runs through many of these books. An essential part of good parenting is to accept and understand your child. Each child is unique, so parenting must be tailored to each child. One child may be more academically inclined than another, another may be athletically gifted, a third may have a passion for art or music.

Each of those children must be nurtured and educated and encouraged along their own path. The same applies to adults. We must accept and understand ourselves before we engage in any program of self-betterment. This reminds me of a quotation often attributed to Einstein, "Everybody is a genius. But if you judge a fish by its ability to climb a tree, it will live its whole life believing that it is stupid."

The process is more complicated with adults because the circumstances of our past may have already interfered with our development. We have the added burden of accepting those circumstances and understanding how they impacted us so we can reverse the damage and prevent it from further inhibiting our growth.

All of these techniques helped me correct some of the dysfunctions that limited my growth and prevented me from achieving happiness and self-fulfillment. However, the first step is the most important—you must accept yourself and your past.

> **Pro Tip:** If I can pass along something I learned, it would be to accept who you are today and accept all the events that have shaped you into the person you are.

What you experience in life, however enjoyable or painful, provides the insight and understanding that lights your path to a brighter future. Your experiences can limit or fuel your growth depending on how you use them. Ignore them or use them as excuses, and they will stunt your growth. Acknowledge them and use them to learn and understand, and they will fuel your growth.

> *What you experience in life, however enjoyable or painful, provides the insight and understanding that lights your path to a brighter future.*

Take the First Step: Self-Acceptance

When I look back on who I was some fifteen years ago and who I am today, I see a huge positive transformation. I am no longer a shrinking violet, anxious and afraid. I now think and act with confidence and intent. I express my views and uncertainties, seek more information when in doubt, fully engage with loved ones, and pursue my dreams. My hope is that you embark on a similar journey that leads to positive transformation in your life.

I am not suggesting that with a small shift in mindset you can be whoever you want to be and do and have whatever you desire. That is not realistic. You may not achieve everything you set your sights on. Life is not a romantic comedy with a tidy, shiny ending.

What is important is that you continue on an upward trajectory that is true to your inner essence so that you can more fully achieve your potential and the highest degree of happiness possible.

For me, the key has been to look at myself in the mirror every day and accept who I am and what happened to me in the past, and to realize that, although I will always carry the memories of that painful past, I have survived it. It has not destroyed me and does not dictate my choices or actions. I made my way through it and—short of death—will survive whatever life throws in my path. You will, too.

Regardless of whether you were neglected, abused, or marginalized in your life, the key to this Fear Dynamics Technique is to embrace who you are today and accept that everything that has happened to you—good and bad—is part of you becoming you. You can make changes to alter your future course, but first you must accept and understand the person you are today.

Imagine a map in the mall with an arrow marked "You Are Here." To get where you want to be, you need to first know where you are. In the context of personal development, it also helps to know how you got to where you are now.

> *Embrace who you are today and accept that everything that has happened to you—good and bad—is part of you becoming you.*

Although cliché, the notion that, "The journey of a thousand miles starts with a single step" (Lao Tzu) is true. The first step on the journey to happiness and self-fulfillment is self-acceptance.

Chapter 2

DAD, THE MOLESTER

My dad was not a nice man. Sometimes when I was sleeping he would sneak into my room and pull all the covers off my bed, ripping me out of a deep sleep. He claimed it was a prank. Another favorite joke of his was to sneak into the bathroom when I was in the shower and dump ice cold water over the shower door onto me. Once again, he glossed over my terror by brushing it off as a hilarious practical joke and mocked my reaction as being overly sensitive.

I never felt safe anywhere in my house; there was no place to hide. I used to sneak off to watch TV alone in the dark basement, but my dad managed to ruin that—by sexually abusing me.

I can write about this now because my parents are deceased. And thanks to years of psychotherapy and reflection, I have, for the most part, moved past the shame. But, as improbable as it may seem, I cannot recall the first time my dad sexually abused me. I have many memories of the abuse happening over the years, but I can't pinpoint the first occurrence.

Some form of emotional and psychological abuse likely was happening my entire life. The physical/sexual abuse phase doesn't have an exact time line, but it ended by the time I was a high school senior.

As an adult, I looked back with a fierce desire to remember and understand, but many facts continued to elude me. As I worked to understand what happened to me, I came to realize that the sexual abuse was not the first step in my father's systematic conditioning and overall psychological and emotional abuse; it was the final step. The sexual element was the culminating stage in my father's subjugation of me and destruction of my self-worth. It is clear to me now that my father was a cunning predator, but I was wholly unaware of that at the time, and for many years later. I actually thought my father cared for me and wanted only the best for me. I looked up to him.

> *What I have come to conclude is that I don't remember the first time because I wasn't there. My body was there, but me—the essence of all I am (or was at the time)—checked out, went on autopilot.*

What I have come to conclude is that I don't remember the first time because I wasn't there. My body was there, but me—the essence of all I am (or was at the time)—checked out, went on autopilot. I know that disconnecting is a well-documented coping mechanism for victims of abuse, but being unable to recall certain events is unpleasant at best and, at worst, disturbing and frightening. I think I had trained myself from infancy to shut down emotionally, to disconnect from the emotional trauma of my household because any reaction on my part was ignored by my parents or worse, sent them into either a rage at my insolence or a narcissistic diatribe about how hard their lives were.

By the time the sexual abuse started, I was able to disconnect with the flip of a switch. Truth be told, I am not sure if I was really ever connected for many years. I do not say this with pride, but to convey how I coped and managed to survive at the time. For the longest time I lived with and relied on this disconnectedness. I've always known that I was abused by my father, but only in the last fifteen years or so have I been able to integrate my experiences, put them into perspective, and comprehend how profoundly they affected me, even years after I physically distanced myself from the dysfunction and abuse.

I didn't tell my mother about the abuse until shortly before she died. If I told her when it was happening, I was certain she would have ignored me or convinced me that I was blowing it out of proportion. Later, I became petrified to my core that if I shared what my father had done to me, either no one would believe me or the whole family would implode, and it would be my fault. The bitter irony of me being afraid that my dysfunctional family would be shattered and have to rebuild is not lost on me; it constantly reminds me of how lost I was and unable to see the reality of my life.

As a kid, I never shared any of this with my siblings. Neither appeared to have had any such issues with Dad, but at the time, we never shared any of our experiences with either parent. Nor did I ever confide in a teacher, guidance counselor, or friend in all my years in school and into my professional life. I alluded to it once or twice with a close friend in college and law school, as well as with my first wife, but never shared it in any real depth until my late thirties. To this day I wonder what I would have said and what would have happened if just one person would have expressed a suspicion that I was being neglected or abused as a child or pushed back against my dismissive behaviors when asked what was bothering me.

The fact that nobody noticed any sign of my inner turmoil or probed for additional information bothers me to this day. It also motivates me to take the time to ask people if they're okay or if there's anything they want to talk about when I see that they may be upset or in distress. I wish someone would have done that for me when I was struggling.

The First Time It Happened?

The earliest recollection I have of being sexually abused by my father transpired in the basement of our home. It was the fall of 1982, and I was in seventh grade. It was my first year out of elementary school, just starting junior high school. Like many houses in central Wisconsin, we had a finished basement. Part of it was our TV room, furnished with two neutral-colored reclining chairs against one wall, a dark beige cloth-patterned couch on the other, and the television along the opposite wall. This room with the TV was at the back of the basement, a short hallway-walk from the fifteen stairs up to the main floor. The basement walls had tiny windows near the top that were at ground level outside, allowing a little ambient light to trickle in during the day.

I had been watching a TV show with my dad. He was sitting on one of the recliners and I was on the couch. When the show went to a commercial break my dad stood up as if he were going to the bathroom or to get something to drink. Instead, he came to the couch and started to poke and tease me, like a brother might do to try to elicit a reaction from a sibling and engage the sibling in a physical contest. My heart began to race, and I knew I didn't like this game. He was laser-focused on me, cajoling me and acting offended when I tried to ignore him.

It felt like the world was shrinking and I could not escape. I realized that I was completely alone with him and nobody was coming to help me. My sister was out with her friends, my brother sound asleep, and my mother oblivious upstairs. I sank into the couch as far as I could, wanting it to swallow me and carry me away. I could not escape. The intensity of "play" quickly escalated when I felt my dad's surprisingly firm hand clamp down on my arm and drag me off the couch onto the carpeted floor. Disengagement was no longer an option. I was on the ground, struggling, trying to get away.

He acted as though this was just some playful wrestling, but I was not a willing participant. I was trying with all my strength not to let him get on top of me and pin me down. I was a kid and much weaker than my dad. I squirmed and clawed to break away, but my efforts were in vain. He was on top. I was being crushed beneath his weight and overwhelmed by his musky smell. He continued to move on top of me, not to pin me or to get me in a wrestling hold, but more as though he was toying with me. He would give me a little room to maneuver to encourage me to try to escape. I would try so hard to get away, but then, effortlessly, he would drag me back and force me again into submission.

With our wriggling and his weight on me, I got a rug burn on my left elbow and shoulder. I remember I showed him my injuries and asked to stop because of them. He said it was nothing and I needed to toughen up and not be a quitter. It was a violent encounter, not in the sense that we broke anything or that physical blows were thrown, but in that my father used his brute force to physically dominate me against my will. I was powerless. No matter how hard I tried, I had no choice. He was in control. I was nothing.

But I didn't give up. I tried again to get away with child-like optimism and then I realized that my shirt was off. He pounced, and I found myself on my back, with my dad ripping off my sweatpants. I fought ferociously to get away, suffering more rug burns. He got me back on my stomach and dropped his full weight on me again.

The wrestling match was intense, bordering on primal. I didn't like what was happening, I didn't like feeling helpless, I didn't like hearing his grunts and feeling the hotness of his breath at the side of my ear, and I didn't like that I could not get him off me no matter how hard I tried. I was trapped. I didn't think to yell for help. I hated it, but I was torn between the belief that my dad could not possibly intentionally harm me in any way and instinctually knowing that this was very wrong.

Suddenly, I felt a wet sensation on my back. I had no idea what it could be. He said nothing. He got off me and stood up, and as I glanced over at him, I was surprised to see him putting on his clothes. I had no idea he had even taken them off. When did that happen? He seemed to be in a daze or drunk. Without a word, he sat back down in his recliner and went back to watching *Magnum P.I.* as if nothing had happened.

I slowly stood up and examined the rug burns on my knees and elbows. I knew something had happened. I put on my sweatpants and shirt, sat back down on the couch, and, like him, returned in silence to watching TV. I just sat there zoned out in front of the TV.

Deep down, I felt the shame of being overpowered and forced to be a part of something I knew instinctually was wrong. At the time, I was too young to understand what had happened. I didn't know much about sex, or masturbation, or ejaculation. I just knew it felt very very wrong, and I was alone.

A Cycle of Abuse

My dad would come to the bedroom I shared with my younger brother. We had bunk beds—mine was the top bunk. On days when my brother would already be up and out of the room and I was still in bed, or if my brother had stayed overnight at a friend's house, my dad would come in and close the door. He would pull me off the top bunk. I would try and grab onto the covers or bed frame, but I would ultimately fall to the floor and the wrestling would begin. He would take me down, I would fight as hard as I could to get him off me, and somehow he would get me shirtless or pantless. He would be on top of me, grunting, then I would feel the wetness. He would quickly dress and leave without uttering a word.

Sometimes he would be naked from the waist down, and other times he would be just in his underwear. Other times, he would follow me down to the river on a hot summer night and demand to skinny dip and then wrestle in the shallow water. I had no safe place. My dad invaded my quiet TV spot, my bedroom, and even the outdoors.

I hated our "game." It was bad enough that my parents made me feel worthless in general, but at least before now they had left me alone. Now my father made sure I had no place to hide and he could do whatever he wanted to me, whenever he wanted. After this started with my dad, I spoke even less at home and with my friends. I felt powerless and cowardly for not standing up against him. I didn't tell anyone because I was ashamed. I thought nobody cared about me, and I deeply doubted that anyone would believe that my father would do this to me.

As much as it still pains me to admit, my father's abuse went on for years. I tried to find ways to get out of these sessions before they started. If we were in the basement watching TV, I would head upstairs to get a drink before a commercial came on and just not return to the basement. For some twisted reason, my father initiated the wrestling pretense only during commercial breaks.

Sometimes I would try the tactic of just lying there and not fighting back. I thought maybe if I didn't fight back, the game would stop or at least end sooner. When I did that, my father would become petulant and whine, "What's wrong with you? We're just having fun." He would scold me for ruining our fun and tell me that I was the weird one for not wanting to play.

Time and time again he would manipulate me into participating in this sick game—me trying to fight him off and then squirming beneath him trying to escape, him catching me one last time, losing our clothes, and the wetness signaling the end. My self-esteem was decimated. I would think, *He's right. This is what we do. This is what we've always done. We wrestle. Why am I ruining it?* After all, it never got to the point of kicking, punching, clawing, or biting. Those seemed to be the unwritten rules of the game and, regardless of how twisted this game was, he was playing by the rules. As hard as I fought back, he never hurt me on the outside. He wanted to control and dominate me and pleasure himself, not cause me physical pain . . . as if that made it okay.

Nowhere to Turn

I lived in abject fear in my own home. I was always anxious. My father was a predator, and my mother was, at best, emotionally distant and detached. It seemed the only attention I received from her was belittlement and rage. I learned to avoid my mother by listening to the sounds of the house. I could tell her footfall compared to that of my siblings and would steer clear. I also knew the sound when my father took his first step on the top stair that led to the basement. Gripped by terror, I would frantically switch the channels to find a movie that was just starting. Sometimes it worked. My dad would fall asleep or my sister would come down or sometimes he would just give up and go upstairs.

I spent as little time as possible at home. I worked as many after-school jobs as I could and spent an inordinate amount of time at my friend Kevin's house, sleeping there as often as possible. I couldn't wait to go to college, but even after I left home I was not completely free. The shame and the regret for not having stood up to my father followed me.

Even in my college and law school years, I was unable to stand up to him. I made a fledgling attempt just after law school, but not until I completely rebuilt my self-esteem and fully understood what had happened to me was I able to finally confront him and let him know the pain he caused me. It took me years to get to that point, but finally I was strong and in control of my life and how I lived. I was confident that regardless of how he responded, I would not be shamed or belittled. I was ready to confront him on my terms.

> *It took me years, but finally I was strong and in control of my life and how I lived.*

My goal was not to dominate him or destroy him. I just wanted to be free from him and not be anything like him. Before he died, I achieved that goal. I finally freed myself from my father and the control he had on my life until well into my adult years. I built my own life and my own family on the foundation of honesty, love, and acceptance.

In this way, I emerged the victor.

CHECKING IN WITH YOUR INNER LITTLE GUY OR GAL

We all enter this world with our own unique personality and special qualities. We are then influenced over time by experience and education. When properly nurtured and nourished, we grow into caring adults. One of life's wonderful gifts is being able to witness this process unfold, especially as parents, teachers, or coaches. Throughout our development, however, I believe our core essence remains constant. I've learned to embrace my core essence, referring to it as "my little guy."

My little guy is the person who I was in my purest form, before the abuse and neglect from my parents. The person who I was since the day I was born. My truest self. As part of my journey, I learned to reconnect with this inner core being. I taught myself to check in with my little guy to see what he thinks and feels. Over the years, I've found him to be a reliable guide. This chapter will dive into the details of this Fear Dynamics Technique.

Just as plants are impacted by the environment in which they grow, our growth and development are impacted by the environment in which we are raised. A plant grown with insufficient sunlight ends up tall, pale, and leggy, desperately pushing its leaves toward a source of light, instead of growing stout and strong and full of foliage. Likewise, children who do not receive the nourishment they need (physically, mentally, emotionally) compensate to protect themselves and attempt to acquire what they need in any way possible. A lack of nurturing and nourishment can result in abnormal growth and development, not just physically, but also mentally and emotionally.

However, deep inside, I believe part of us remains the same from the day we were born. Just as our genes define our potential for physical and mental development, I believe each of us has a core essence that defines our potential in respect to personality and emotional development. Regardless of whether a child is neglected or is raised in a loving, caring family, that child's core essence remains untouched. It may be buried under learned behaviors and struggle to be heard, but it survives. This is the inner little guy that I connect with on an emotional level to get at my core and unabashed feelings.

> *My little guy is the person who I was in my purest form.*

We are products of the interaction of our genetic makeup, our core essence, and the environment in which we were raised— nature *and* nurture and something else indescribable we have not yet discovered. None of these three factors alone defines us or determines our destiny. Freedom of choice ultimately gives us tremendous power to change the course of our trajectory and become the people we want to be.

I believe that our only destiny in this life is to fulfill the potential contained in our core essence, and to do that, we need to discover and understand what that core essence is, who we really are inside—the little guy (or gal) inside you, the person untainted by life, the genuine version of yourself.

> *Just as plants are impacted by the environment in which they grow, our growth and development are impacted by the environment in which we are raised.*

Losing Myself

Have you ever felt so burdened by life, so used and abused that you started to miss yourself and wonder whatever happened to you? Maybe life seemed to be going well and then, slowly, almost unnoticeably, it became burdensome, and the light inside you became dimmer and dimmer. What happened?

This happened to me so early in my life that I didn't know how bright the light inside could be until I was in my late thirties. For most of my life I never felt worthy or valuable. At my core I believed I was not deserving of anyone's time, attention, or—at a core level—love. I did not believe I was valuable enough for anyone to listen to me or even notice me. I grew up feeling as though I was a waste of my parents' time.

Many of the myriad instances when my father made me feel worthless are foggy in my memory, but I had an experience watching my son and father interact that was emblematic of my childhood existence and transported me immediately back in time to the feelings of worthlessness I had as a little guy.

When my son, Nick, was about three years old, my dad and his second wife visited us in Colorado. We had brunch at a resort in Colorado Springs called The Broadmoor and were walking around when my son announced he wanted to play "Hide and Seek." Nick ran and crouched behind a rock up ahead on the path and put his head down. As we approached the rock, Nick was clearly visible, but he kept his head down because he was three and really into the game. When we were about even with the rock, my dad bellowed out to Nicholas, "We can see you by the rock," and just kept on walking—didn't even break stride. Crushing. My. Spirit.

> *Freedom of choice ultimately gives us tremendous power to change the course of our trajectory and become the people we want to be.*

I could feel the palpable anger rise in my throat at his dismissal of my son, but also for the years of his dismissal of me. I instantly felt the shame of disappointing my dad—I could not even play "Hide and Seek" correctly. Of course, I didn't say anything to him. Luckily, this mistreatment was out of the ordinary in my son's experience, so I assume his toddler brain simply concluded that Grandpa was a real buzzkill. My dad could not pass up any opportunity to shame, belittle, or silence whomever he chose as his target. The saddest aspect of this is that I do not believe my dad even thought about what he was doing. It was second nature behavior for him.

Unfortunately, my mother also made me feel worthless, albeit in other creative ways. Regardless of whether she was drunk or sober, her attention would drift away from me while I was talking, even if she had asked me a question. Sometimes, I would stop talking mid-sentence and I would wait for her to say, "Go on . . ." but she never did.

Once, when I was around thirteen, my friend Kevin spent the night (which was a rarity). I was in the bathroom going through my nightly routine of washing my face and brushing my teeth. I went out to the living room to say good night to my mom, and she went on and on about what a great job Kevin did brushing his teeth and how I should be more like Kevin. What was weird (or not so weird) is that Kevin hadn't brushed his teeth yet; the person she saw brushing his teeth was *me*. It was just Mom's subtle way of letting me know I was not good enough; she actually believed I wasn't capable of mastering basic oral hygiene.

On another occasion, when I learned that I had made it to the later rounds for the Rhodes Scholarship competition my senior year of college, instead of being proud of me, my mom's response was "Why didn't you make it to the final 32?" I was disappointed I did not get to the final group, but I was proud of my effort and the work I had put in to make it to that point in the process.

Instead of nurturing me to grow and develop fully into the person I had the potential to become, my parents succeeded in stunting my emotional development and crushing my self-esteem. I became less and less of myself until I could no longer recognize the person I really was—the little guy inside me who wanted to live life fully was lost, alone, and cowering in the dark.

Getting to Know You

The fear-and-shame boat is crowded with all of us, so in an effort to help you get off the boat and explore the shore, I want to pass along some techniques that have helped me deal with fear dynamics. My therapist and I developed a practice of connecting with my inner child—my most authentic self. I call this, "Checking in with the little guy."

You can call your inner child any name you prefer—I suggest you choose a name that brings you some comfort, or feel free to use "little guy" or "little gal" or some other nickname. While this method may sound corny, it was, and still is, a great tool I use to connect with my deepest emotions and most honest thoughts. I think of my little guy as myself before I was burdened with fear, anxiety, and shame. He is a pure being who easily connects with his thoughts and emotions and can move freely between having a feeling and expressing it. He is my core essence. Whenever I connect with him, my body warms, and my emotions flow more easily.

When you access your inner child, you can get to your most authentic self and identify your unvarnished thoughts and feelings. I touch base with my little guy on a regular basis to get a read on my inner emotions that I may push down from the surface because I don't want to deal with my feelings when I am afraid or ashamed of them. I also find time to be with him when I am overwhelmed with my adult life and responsibilities and am feeling lost or directionless. I have learned to trust and depend on my interactions with the little guy to help me sort out situations I find emotionally complicated or unclear.

Pro Tip: To get in touch with your inner child, first enter a relaxed state and let your mind wander.

Often, I check in with my little guy when I am running because it is a time I have with few distractions and interruptions and the rhythm helps me to stay calm. I also find that sitting in a quiet place with a notepad and pen to jot down thoughts is very helpful for interacting with my little guy.

> *When you access your inner child,*
> *you can get to your most authentic*
> *self and identify your unvarnished*
> *thoughts and feelings.*

Next, focus on a situation in which you are searching for clarity or understanding of your thoughts and feelings. For example, we were considering moving to a different home. I had a lot of mixed feelings and thoughts about this prospective change. I was plagued by questions like, "Why do I want to move?" "Do I need to move?" "Do I deserve a nicer house?" "Is moving to a new house right for our family?" I use my connection with my little guy to get at my most honest, unvarnished emotional reaction to these questions. He's not a rational guy; he's an emotional guy. The purpose of connecting with the little guy is not to evaluate a decision—that comes later. It is to access genuine emotions about a situation or question.

Maybe it's a new job or a new project at work. Maybe it's deciding whether or where to go on vacation. Maybe you had a disagreement with a loved one that you are trying to sort through. *You can insert your own issue and questions here.* Do your best to relax while you are musing on any questions that pop up around the situation you are contemplating.

As I mull over these questions and issues that pop into my head, I will check in with my little guy to see how he is feeling. I'll say to myself, "What do you think about us moving to a new home?" I'll ask my little guy, "Do you want to move?" If I have a writing pad, I will write down whatever answers and insights my little guy shares. I do not filter the thoughts that come into mind. While I am in this contemplative state, I write down every thought or feeling or idea I have.

> The purpose of connecting with the
> little guy is not to evaluate a decision—
> that comes later. It is to access genuine
> emotions about a situation or question.

I keep asking myself questions and ruminating over my answers either in my head or by writing them down. When I feel as though I have covered all my concerns about the issue, I will take some deep breaths and thank my little guy for being so honest and open. I try to honor this process and let myself feel safe while I engage in it.

Last, I review whatever I have written down. When you first begin this process, it may be most helpful to record your thoughts either in writing or by recording voice memos because it's easier to review your thoughts and ideas when you have some record of them. I reflect on what I have written and see whether it feels true to me at this time and place in my life. Usually, it does.

This technique enables me to connect with my inner self to discover what I really feel, and it helps me sort out my feelings on a wide variety of topics and issues. It helps in personal relationships, as well as professional ones. I believe it is a core aspect of healing from my childhood trauma because I am finally validating myself. Now, my little guy knows that his thoughts and feelings are important, that they matter to me as an adult, and I utilize him as a guide. I listen and care about what my little guy thinks and feels—something I wish my parents had done for me.

This sounds simple and basic, but the foundational self-esteem and self-comfort created from this process is truly staggering. I suggest getting to know your own inner child as you continue on your path to overcoming the fear and anxiety that stand in the way of your happiness and self-fulfillment. It may seem impossible to advocate for or protect your adult self, but it is almost effortless to act to protect a child.

Pro Tip: Make a point to validate your inner self, and you will be happier and more comfortable with nearly every decision you make because you are advocating for and protecting yourself.

FEAR DYNAMICS TECHNIQUE #3

MAKE EYE CONTACT

For the better part of my life, I avoided eye contact. For me, I was almost always operating from a place of fear or shame. I was afraid that if I were to connect with someone through eye contact as we spoke, the person would recognize me as a fraud, or worse, discern my inner vulnerabilities and use them against me. The possibility of eye contact was a source of fear, a certainty that I would be opening myself up to something painful. I realized early on in my self-help journey that if I wasn't looking someone in the eye, there was something going on that I needed to examine. Next time you realize you are avoiding eye contact, pause and think about what is scaring you. Making eye contact is Fear Dynamics Technique #3.

Going way back, I even took a step beyond not looking people in the eye by actively avoiding human contact. When I was in law school, the main building had two exits. One was through the atrium, an area full of tables and chairs and people hanging out between classes. The other was down an enclosed hallway. Guess which path I took? Yes, the hallway. I fled the building as though I was being chased, all in an effort to avoid any "stop and chats" along the way.

> *Next time you realize you are avoiding eye contact, pause and think about what is scaring you.*

This is emblematic of how I approached all social settings—*avoidance*. I may have been alone most of the time, but at least I was safe. After law school I was required to attend business events that necessitated some social interaction. I delivered my polite, canned responses but rarely connected in any genuine way with people. The next day, I wouldn't be able to remember anyone I met, and I suspect that the people I met did not remember me. So much for successful networking.

As I got older and started to understand and integrate my current self with my past self through psychotherapy and introspection, I realized the crucial importance of eye contact. First, when you look someone in the eye, it forces you to be present in that moment. Think about it—you can't look someone in the eye and be thinking about where the nearest exit is. Disconnecting emotionally and mentally while maintaining eye contact is nearly impossible. Also, maintaining eye contact helps the other person stay engaged too, because as long as you are engaging with their eyes, they cannot disconnect.

Eye contact cements human connection. To engage in open, honest, and authentic communication with loved ones, colleagues, adversaries, friends, and even passers-by, you must be present, and one of the best ways to force yourself to do that is to look people in the eye when you are talking to them. I know it is hard, but so worth the effort.

> *When you look someone in the eye, it forces you to be present in that moment.*

When our son was young, we learned the critical importance of communicating with children at eye level—crouching, kneeling, or sitting, so that we were physically at the same level as our son. By doing so, we conveyed the message that he is as important as us and that what he had to say mattered.

Pro Tip: Even such a small change in perspective and perception can do an amazing job at forging self-worth. These seeds of self-esteem are easy to plant in children, and we need to nourish them in ourselves.

He is now taller than both my wife and me, but we all still look at each other in the eye and try to stay connected when we talk. Conveying mutual respect is a bond that helped to keep us together through the teen years and now the adult ones as our son progresses through the stages of independence. Acknowledging the importance of looking people in the eye is relatively easy with children, but we need to remind ourselves that everyone deserves to be treated as equals, and deserves the same level of engagement. I am a huge advocate of looking people in the eye when interacting with them. It makes a massive difference in your connection with the world.

Start with Casual Encounters

If you tend to avoid eye contact for whatever reason, I strongly recommend you practice making and maintaining eye contact until it is natural and comfortable for you to do so. Keep in mind that eye contact should be natural; you are not challenging the person to a staring contest. Feel free to blink and let your eyes wander a little to the person's forehead, chin, cheeks, and so on.

I suggest starting this technique with everyday encounters. For example, when a server at a local restaurant is taking your order or when a cashier hands you your receipt, try to make eye contact, and give them a genuine, "Thank you." As you become more comfortable and confident in these casual, short-term interactions, practice with colleagues at work. For example, when you greet a coworker or hand someone a file folder then look the person in the eye.

I started by practicing with my assistant. I did not sit her down and say, "Don't freak out, but from now on I'm going to look you in the eye when we speak." I just started doing it. Instead of yelling over the cubicle, I would walk over to her desk, address her by her name, and maintain eye contact when we spoke. The results were quickly apparent. In the past, she would listen to me but not look up and often continue to do whatever she was doing and then acknowledge that she heard me, all without ever looking at me. Often, I would then get an email asking for clarification on the task because either my request was unclear, or she did not digest the full scope of the direction. As soon as I started to look her in the eye, she would have to stop what she was doing and focus on our interaction.

We were both present, and this effort enhanced our communication which resulted in us working together more effectively and efficiently. If it would make you more comfortable to let people know that you are going to be practicing on them, that is a valid approach as well. The key to this technique is practice, however you choose to start.

Move Up to More Challenging Situations

As soon as these casual interactions become second nature, you will find it easier to establish eye contact while communicating with other people, such as your spouse, boss, or client/customer. I strive to maintain eye contact in every personal encounter. It wasn't easy at first, and in all honesty, I still struggle in situations when I am advocating for myself or if I am feeling misunderstood or challenged. For me, the more emotional the situation, the greater the challenge to genuinely engage. Eye contact makes us feel vulnerable, especially in situations in which we feel threatened or we anticipate a negative response or reaction. This makes it more difficult to sustain the connection, but it is well worth the effort.

When speaking with my wife or son, I want to be certain that they know I care about them. Specifically, being able to maintain eye contact with my wife after I hurt her feelings is challenging, but it is crucially important to intentionally and firmly re-establishing our relationship of trust, whether the disruption is large or small. We felt that this quick reconnection by making eye contact with each other was so effective, my wife and I created a practice of pausing and looking into each other's eyes for five seconds or so before bed. It doesn't have to be some weird mind-meld experience—we might smile, talk, hug, or be quiet. The point is that we establish an intimate connection on a regular basis.

This moment helps us feel connected in our relationship before we go to sleep each night. We also try to do this when I come home from work at night and after not seeing each other for a while due to travel or other obligations. It is a quick and easy way to reconnect with someone important. Sometimes we may drift apart for a few days because of the stresses of life and then, hopefully, one of us notices and we take the time to reconnect again with eye contact. Being intentional and taking a moment to look each other in the eye helps to reforge a bond. It is a tiny habit, but massively important and powerful.

Pro Tip: Try this technique with someone you love.

At first it might feel like the most uncomfortable exercise in the world to stand there and just look another person in the eye without speaking for even a few seconds. However, the benefits vastly outweigh the uneasiness, and over time the discomfort fades. In that moment, you shut out all concerns in the world around you and become the most important *everything* to each other. The connection will be something that you look forward to, and if for some reason you do not, that is a signal that something is likely off.

I know that when operating from a place of fear and anxiety it can be daunting to think about looking people in the eye, but I do believe it will bring only positive results to your life. Ultimately, it will make you feel less nervous in social encounters and more grounded in professional interactions. Practicing eye contact is like exposure therapy—you increase your exposure to whatever makes you anxious until it no longer triggers anxiety or until you can manage the anxiety.

> *Being intentional and taking a moment to look each other in the eye helps to reforge a bond. It is a tiny habit, but massively important and powerful.*

Another reason to work on maintaining eye contact is that even though you may be avoiding eye contact out of fear, others may interpret your reluctance to look them in the eye as your attempt to hide the truth, which is probably exactly what you are doing. However, they may perceive you as untrustworthy or disingenuous. Or they may assume you are being standoffish because you feel you are superior to them or that you simply dislike them. Here is a vignette of how fear dynamics can play out:

I'm not looking you in the eye because I am afraid. You think I am not looking you in the eye because I am aloof (at best) or trying to lie to you (at worst). You won't look me in the eye now because I have, unknown to me, insulted you. We both leave this encounter feeling negative toward each other and wary of the next encounter.

Consider the impact eye contact has on others. Looking people in the eye makes them feel respected, appreciated, and heard. When you make eye contact, it lets people know that you genuinely want to engage with them. If you show people you respect them and respect their time, they will respect you and your time as well. This Fear Dynamics Technique will lead to more genuine and meaningful communication and, likely, more productive and fulfilling professional and personal relationships. I find it especially powerful for establishing trust in professional settings, when it is vital to establish it quickly.

Looking people in the eye makes them feel respected, appreciated, and heard. When you make eye contact, it lets people know that you genuinely want to engage with them.

Regardless of how emotionally uncomfortable you may feel looking someone in the eye, you can do this.

Pro Tip: Start small and keep working on it. The more you practice, the more comfortable you will become.

Soon, it will no longer be a grind but become second nature. In addition, you will begin to reap the rewards of engaging on a deeper level with the people around you, which is a great incentive to drive your forward progress.

FEAR DYNAMICS TECHNIQUE #4

BUILD IN A PAUSE

One of the most valuable nuggets of wisdom I offer in this book is reflected in a song by Simon & Garfunkel, an American folk-rock duo that was one of the best-selling music groups in the 1960s. I have little doubt that you have heard someone, somewhere, sing or hum one of their biggest hits—"The Sound of Silence," "Mrs. Robinson," "Bridge Over Troubled Water," or "Homeward Bound." But the song that contains the advice I offer comes from one of their sillier songs, "The 59th Street Bridge Song," commonly known as the "Feelin' Groovy" song. The lyrics start like this: "Slow down, you move too fast . . . You got to make the morning last . . ." I suggest that we—the anxiety-ridden—sing this song to ourselves several times over the course of every day. So, here's your first homework assignment: Google this song and listen to it closely.

I'm not suggesting we skip down the street, throw off all of our daily obligations and watch the grass grow. What I am saying is—and I cannot stress this enough—*S-l-o-w d-o-w-n*. I want to emphasize this point as strenuously as I can. I believe we rush through the moments of our day, doing three or more things at once—looking at our phone, listening to a colleague, thinking about getting to a meeting in fifteen minutes, and now, Googling "The 59th Street Bridge Song" . . . Stop it! *Slow down.* Take a breath. I don't mean to preach (or nag), but slowing down will make a huge difference in your happiness and satisfaction, and it can make you far more effective and efficient in all you do.

> I cannot stress this enough:
> S-l-o-w d-o-w-n.

Let's look specifically at slowing down your reactions to life situations. For me, conversations are minefields fraught with internal trepidation and the anticipation of danger at every turn—people asking me questions, my opinion or—heaven forbid—my feelings. Here's a simple conversation from my past: My wife asked, (with the ordinary interest of a Monday night), "What would you like for dinner?" I replied (palms sweating despite the innocent nature of this query), "I don't care. Whatever you want."

Psychoanalyzing this from my perspective, I responded this way because my non-existent self-esteem and omnipresent self-doubt had conditioned me to believe I was unworthy to express a preference on even so innocent of a topic. From my wife's perspective, I was a complete jackass who couldn't be bothered to weigh in on any decisions in our household, from the inconsequential to the major. The added bonus to this counterproductive behavior was that by agreeing to what I didn't like, didn't want, or felt as though I had no control over, I was sowing seeds of discontent that would eventually lead me to act out passive-aggressively to my wife—charming, I know.

I was guilty of the same behavior at work. Simple questions triggered anxiety attacks accompanied by racing heartbeat, flushed face, sweaty palms, and a nearly overwhelming desire to escape. To cope, I perfected the perfunctory response—wishy-washy, safe, and half-hearted. The internal pressure my brain inflicted on me drove me to be reactive in conversations, hurrying my responses to speed the discussion to an end. I would be so preoccupied with what I had just said, trying to ensure it was correct and considering the possible ramifications of my response, I would barely hear the person's response, and then I was expected to respond again. If I could just exit the conversation without saying something that the other person may not like or that revealed me to be a fraud, that was success, and I felt safe.

I was internally agitated all the time, in a constant state of *undifferentiated anxiety* (I was anxious about everything and I could not pinpoint the cause of my anxiety). I am not exaggerating. I would wake up each morning humming with anxiety, even before I had my first conscious thought about what daily tasks lie ahead of me. I would be gripped with fear, but completely unaware of its source as I swung my legs over the side of the bed.

For most of my life I assumed everyone woke up with a paralyzing feeling in their chest. I assumed it was part of the human condition. This was one of the first things I tackled in therapy. First, I needed to figure out where this anxiety was coming from. Then I needed to understand how I could manage my anxiety and how to regularly dissipate it during my daily home and work life.

> *The internal pressure my brain inflicted on me drove me to be reactive in conversations, hurrying my responses to speed the discussion to an end.*

Understanding the Roots of My Fear and Trepidation

Growing up, I was trained to believe that what I said did not matter and that my voice could not and would not be heard. This false world view contributed to my anxiety and my struggle to thoughtfully engage in conversation. My mother humorously used to tell an anecdote about how I didn't speak until I was almost three years old and that she was concerned about my cognitive development.

My theory to explain my delayed verbal communication is that as I lay in my crib and my cries went unheeded, as my emotional needs went unmet, I gave up trying early on. It was a lost cause. Nobody heard. Nobody listened. Nobody was coming. Not only did this negatively impact my desire to engage with the world, it also slowly and systematically eroded my sense of self-worth.

Even after I began to speak, the message I received from my parents was that my words didn't matter. My father treated me with complete disregard. When I say he ignored my words, I mean it literally. I would say something to him in a clear audible voice and he would pretend that I hadn't said a word. Any conversation I initiated was met with vague nods, indifferent responses, or utter disregard. On the rare occasion he did acknowledge something I said, it usually was to ridicule me and my ideas.

I recall when I was in elementary school coming home and being asked by my mother how my day was. Before a word escaped my lips, my father interjected immediately, "First, I woke up, then I got out of bed, then I went to the bathroom, then I went to the kitchen," ripping through this litany and mocking me about the level of detail I had given in the past. I quickly learned that my thoughtful answers were unwelcome.

This was not an isolated incident. He systematically heaped humiliation on me. Whenever he was around and someone asked me a question about my day, he responded with virtually identical words and derision. He did this even when I was an adult. He never asked how my day was but entered the conversations I was having with others to make sure I knew he did not care and that others should not waste their time talking to me. I grew up thinking I was never right and had no value as a person. I came to believe that no one cared about my feelings or opinions and that if I were brave enough to express them, either I would be ignored, humiliated, or disparaged.

Given this backdrop, authority figures create some interesting dynamics for me, and the world is filled with authority figures—bosses, parents, spouses, customers, clients, even the auto mechanic, restaurant server, and veterinarian have some control over you in their realms. Interactions and anticipated interactions with authority figures were steeped in irrational fear for me.

I could not even be comfortable in the role of an authority figure because I never wanted anyone to feel how I used to feel under my first and most powerful authority figure—my father. Instead of bolstering me and making me feel invincible (which is what good fathers do), he made me feel worthless, powerless, and insignificant. I grew up petrified of what people—especially those in authority—would think of me, certain they would view me as the apprehensive, ignorant, good-for-nothing son.

After I was able to recognize my struggles with anxiety and fear, I realized I didn't know how to respond to simple questions or situations without feeling like I was being attacked or ignored. I needed to create a method to respond to questions in a healthy and productive way. The first hurdle I worked to clear was slowing down my mind and getting a handle on my physical responses to the emotionally-driven anxiety. I realized if I could just slow down the situation, I could assess my feelings and the other person's actual intent and then produce a thoughtful and meaningful response. I worked hard to eliminate a canned response, and the way I succeeded was by building in a pause. The concept of this Fear Dynamics Technique is simple but putting it into practice can be a challenge. Master it, and you will feel more connected, relaxed, and confident in your daily interactions.

> *The concept of slowing down is simple but putting it into practice can be a challenge. Master it, and you will feel more connected, relaxed, and confident in your daily interactions.*

Training Yourself to Build in a Pause

The first step of this technique of building in a pause is to *slow down*, thereby slowing the pace of everything around you. Give yourself time to think and act without feeling rushed or pressured.

Taking time to pause and not be disruptive to the natural flow of life is easier said than done. Here is the method I use:

1. Consciously say, sing, or think to yourself, "Slow down, you move too fast."
2. Put into action these four simple words—*Build in a pause.*

I know it sounds easy, but it takes focus and effort. If you can master building in a pause before you respond in nearly every situation, you are likely to see a massive positive change in all your relationships and in your daily interactions with everyone. Whenever someone asks a question or you feel compelled to express yourself, slow down, take a breath, a pause, a moment. It's okay to do in any situation. In fact, it will likely improve your reaction to every stimulus or provocation the universe provides.

Sometimes all you may need is a nanosecond. It is amazing how quickly the brain processes input and computes an appropriate response. A pause that may be imperceptible to the people around you can be a game changer in how you respond. Often times in dealing with our teenage son I found it helpful to build in a pause. Even though my initial internal reaction to his request for an expensive new gaming system may be, "What are you crazy, you just got a gaming system . . ." When I build in a pause, I can realize that I'm applying my own upbringing, where I was denied nearly every request by my parents. Then I can assess his request a little more rationally.

Importantly, the pause not only slows me down, but my pause demonstrates to my son that I am willing to think about his questions and requests and that I do not just react and shut down every idea he has. So this has a doubly beneficial impact on our relationship and creates a foundation for positive future interactions and expectations. An added layer of benefit is it may teach my son to pause in other situations he is in, as he may be more likely to get a meaningful interaction from others if he slows down.

> *Building in a pause can help you avoid the fear dynamics of the ping-pong fight: One comment escalates into a fight because the other person feels attacked and responds with an aggressive comment, and so on.*

By building in a pause, you suppress the instinct to jab at the other person who may have made a hurtful comment that would otherwise escalate a mundane conversation into a vicious verbal sparring match. Even more beneficial, a pause enables you to reflect on your reaction to a situation and consider the possible consequences of your options. If you exist in a fear/anxiety prism, your reactions can be irrational and therefore inappropriate to the situation. We have all observed someone overreact to a situation and wondered why that person behaved that way. Often, we chalk it up to the person being a jerk, and to the outside world, that is likely a fair statement. We do not understand the internal processes producing the outward behavior.

If this person built in a pause and considered a rational response, he probably would not have lashed out and would have responded in a more measured way that may have actually produced a positive result for all involved. Building in a pause can help you avoid the fear dynamics of the ping-pong fight: One comment escalates into a fight because the other person feels attacked and responds with an aggressive comment, and so on.

Stop Being Defensive

When you are anxious and afraid, you are perpetually on the defensive. At least I was. Before I adopted the practice of building in a pause, I felt as though almost anything anyone said to me was an attack or that it was a way of baiting me into a fight. I had been led to believe that my very existence needed to be justified and that any question about my thoughts or actions was a personal assault on me. I believed I needed to defend myself against these attacks or suppress the vicious anger I was feeling. Even during casual interactions, I felt that people were engaging with me in an aggressive manner.

> *A pause enables you to reflect on your reaction to a situation and consider the possible consequences of your options.*

This mindset was real and fully ingrained in me. That reality, coupled with my anxiety, made it nearly impossible for me to have calm, healthy conversations with anyone. Always on defense, I was wired to perceive that whoever was engaging with me was out to personally defeat me. For example, when I felt criticized or reprimanded by my wife (sometimes justifiably), I would either completely disengage or unconsciously jab at her with a quick snide remark to get her to back off, just as a boxer jabs at his opponent to keep him at a safe distance while gradually weakening him.

Ours was an especially harmful dynamic because we knew each other so well; each of us knew exactly what to say to inflict the most pain. Feeling the sting, she responded in kind, and the conversation would soon become a bitter, verbal boxing match, ending in a draw and leaving both of us bruised and battered emotionally. These kind of fear dynamics exchanges can be avoided by building in a pause.

If you struggle with anxiety, slowing down and building in a pause is essential. But even if you are not always on the defensive, building in a pause can lead to more thoughtful interactions with everyone in virtually all situations. Essentially, it requires that one party take the initiative to grab the ping-pong ball or ring the bell to cease the conflict and give everyone a chance to regain his or her composure. My wife and I used this technique frequently with our teenaged son. My wife found it particularly effective to take a pause before she responded to a text from him asking for permission to do something that she thought was semi-outrageous, but he thought was a no-brainer in the yes column.

I often use this technique in professional settings when someone makes a completely unrealistic proposition—which seemingly occurs daily. When I am on a call or in a meeting and one person tries to push an agenda or a position, I build in a pause and remind myself, *You don't have to say anything, you don't have to do anything.*

Pro Tip: Remember to *slow down* and take a breath, a pause, a moment. It's okay—you don't need permission, and nobody can force an immediate response from you.

This technique does not need to interrupt the flow of interaction. I am not suggesting a big production is always needed to create this pause; it can occur in the blink of an eye once you master the technique. This is an internal moment for yourself. Nobody even has to know. It can be your secret.

> *Building in a pause can lead to more thoughtful interactions with everyone in virtually all situations.*

I have learned that it's okay for me to build in a pause at a restaurant if I am feeling pressured by the server or by my fellow diners to place my order. Now that I am more willing and able to be in touch with my desires and beliefs, I realize I have the right to think calmly and clearly. Sometimes it takes me a bit to decide what I want to order and that's okay for me. It's okay for you, too. If you are concerned about the server, just say you need more time.

> *I realize I have the right to think calmly and clearly.*

Sometimes you may need more than a momentary pause, and it's perfectly acceptable to take a few moments. You can always say, "Hold on a sec, please give me a moment to think." At one time in my life, saying something like that was almost unimaginable. My first thought was, *I could never say that.* It shows weakness, and it will be used against me. In addition, I was so unaccustomed to taking care of myself that if I did actually take the time to assess my needs, all my pent-up rage at the world would explode, and I would probably scream something at the person awaiting my response and add an expletive or two.

I speak from experience. I have torn into someone who did not deserve it because I was trying to pause and became overwhelmed by the emotions that flooded in when I paused to consider my needs. I had to practice a great deal before I was comfortable enough to routinely request a moment to think and to use that moment productively.

I have three tips for easing into this Fear Dynamics Technique:

1. Practice at home or with friends in low-pressure situations.
2. Let people know that you are going to be practicing this technique. Sometimes, practice is easier when others are aware of the change you are trying to make. It's like letting people know you're trying to be healthier, so they understand why you're having fruit for dessert instead of that fudge brownie.
3. Practice asking for a moment to think even if you really don't need it. It will become part of what people expect from you, so when you need it, it is available.

Keep practicing. It is exactly like creating muscle memory so that your mind subconsciously requests a moment whenever you need more time to think or feel. Building in a pause—no matter how long—will help you make better, more thoughtful choices. This tiny habit has significantly improved my relationships and interactions with others in both casual and high-pressure settings, and helps me almost every day to avoid getting entrenched in fear dynamics. I strongly urge you to adopt it.

Chapter 3

MOM, THE ALCOHOLIC

Although my father was a cunning sexual predator, when he abused me he almost followed a code. He had a routine and rules of engagement. In contrast, my mother had no rules. Living with her was like sitting on a ticking time bomb. She was sure to explode; we just never knew when. We could never predict who or what would set her off or how loud and long the blasts would last. When she wasn't spewing vitriol, she moved through the house like a ghost of herself, absent from her body and the rest of us.

A Functioning Alcoholic . . . Functional at Work, Anyway

My mom was a functioning alcoholic, at least within the realm of her profession. She drank most nights, far more heavily on Friday and Saturday when she didn't have to work the next morning. When she drank, everyone in the house walked on eggshells. This created a high baseline level of anxiety present at all times. Even my father would steer clear of her, and for good reason. When she decided to dish out invectives, hatred, and anger, few could do it better. She was a highly intelligent wordsmith. Her insults flew toward their targets like guided missiles. I've never heard anyone speak with such personalized and effective malice.

My mother didn't keep her utter disappointment with her life to herself or release it within the privacy of her relationship with my dad. I was frequently present for my mom's verbal lashings of my dad. She would tell him how disappointed she was in her life, in him, in their life together. She freely expressed how much she regretted marrying him and that she should have married someone else. It got worse from there, and neither seemed concerned that my siblings and me—their children— were taking it all in.

Mom was unhappy being married to Dad and being part of our family, and everyone needed to be reminded of the fact that she could have done much better with her life. I knew from a very young age that my mother would rather have been someplace else, been someone else . . . She was profoundly unhappy, distant, emotionally unreachable.

My father, to my constant surprise, would rarely match my mother insult for insult. He would either disregard her or acquiesce. Ignoring what she said was an incredible trick because it involved subtly signaling that he had heard her but chose not to respond, neither agreeing nor disagreeing. Of course, my mom found his ploy maddening, so she just cranked up the volume, going along with the ruse that he just hadn't heard her.

During these engagements I saw my dad as a master flute player mesmerizing a poisonous serpent. His skill at seeming to listen and understand while simultaneously completely ignoring my mom would be the stuff of legend if it were not such a horrific way to treat another human being, especially one he supposedly loved.

> *I saw my dad as a master flute player mesmerizing a poisonous serpent.*

One wrong move though, and my dad was toast. I would suddenly hear my mom screaming at him at the top of her voice. I couldn't always decipher what she said, but her tone signaled the beginning of the end of the battle. Gradually, her voice would trail off, and a tense silence would permeate the home.

I never witnessed my father get physically violent with my mother or vice versa, but my mother would lose control. Her violence was a force of nature, stumbling around uncontrolled, throwing glasses, breaking ashtrays. I didn't see her in action, but I heard the storm and wandered out of my bedroom on several Saturday mornings to assess the damage from the night before.

My dad wasn't my mom's only target. She was an equal-opportunity abuser of all her children as well, and her personal attacks against me further eroded my already flagging self-esteem. Throughout childhood and young adulthood, I experienced waves of hating my mother and wanting her gone. I know this is a familiar theme among children of alcoholics.

What I find fascinating is that even though intellectually I considered my mother's neglect and abuse to be the lesser of two evils in our home, for a long time I was much more open and active in my hatred of her than of my father. I was able to push her away emotionally and join my family's bandwagon of trashing her, all the while keeping the secret about my dad. After my parent's divorce, I'd visit my dad and talk to him regularly. For some reason, I participated in that relationship but worked stridently to completely distance myself from my mother.

She Tried

Now, I view my mother in a softer light. As the years passed and my relationship with my parents evolved, I became more sensitive to a deep distinction between my parents—one that drives me to empathize with my mother more now than I ever did in my early life. Unlike my father, my mother demonstrated an ability to look at her life objectively and tried to change her circumstances and improve. She never outwardly expressed any accountability for her shortcomings or mistakes (at least to me), but she did work to change her life for the better.

> *Throughout childhood and young adulthood, I experienced waves of hating my mother and wanting her gone. I know this is a familiar theme among children of alcoholics.*

After she retired, she moved to Florida and became active in her community, regularly volunteering to save sea turtle eggs and working at a local museum. She also tried to have some relationship with our son when he was young by writing him sweet notes and cards. In contrast, my father avoided and rejected any personal accountability for his actions or the damage he caused, even on his deathbed when it was too late for redemption. This one difference between my parents is huge in my mind. This isn't to say that my mother's words and actions early in my life hurt or damaged me any less, but I do appreciate that she recognized a need for change at some point and made an effort to do so later in her life.

When I look back on my childhood through a healthier lens, I can see how my father also victimized my mother with his need to dominate and to project superiority. As my mother spiraled into alcoholism, he did nothing to help her. Instead, he did his best to convince us that he was the dependable parent and that she was useless and to be reviled. He dismissed and ignored my mother in a subtle way that I am sure not only infuriated her, but also hurt her deeply. My dad could defend his actions and claim he was listening to her, but I believe it was all an attempt to marginalize my mother while elevating his own sense of self-importance.

After my parents divorced following my mother's forced rehab in 1989, she tried to reconnect with me over the years with care packages, cards, and phone calls. Her efforts were forced, and I was still so embittered that I was unable to acknowledge her clumsy gestures without rage. During my second year of law school, she sent me a large box at Christmas. I can't tell you what was inside because I didn't open it. I returned it with a note stating that I did not want whatever she was sending. My roommate was aghast at my actions. To not even look at a package from my mother and reject it summarily was unfathomable to him. And now I see its cruelty too.

Over the next several years, my mother regularly sent cards and notes and tried to be supportive. I never completely cut her out of my life, but I kept her at a great distance. I did not invite her to my wedding after law school in 1995 and barely let her know where I was living. I kept her informed out of some familial duty rather than any affection. Then a test presented itself.

Getting to Know My Mother

In the winter of 1999, my mother, still living and working in Stevens Point, Wisconsin, broke her hip curling. Yes, curling—the sport you may have seen only on early morning weekday broadcasts of the winter Olympics. Curling is sort of a wintery combination of bocce ball and shuffleboard that is played on ice with a broom. Not the smartest sport for a frail woman in her 60s, but that's how she chose to spend social time and stay in shape. Regardless, my mother was struggling and had no one to help her move out of the hospital and back into her apartment. I found it sad that she had lived in Stevens Point for more than thirty years and had no local friends or family she could call to help.

> *Yes, curling—the sport you may have seen only on early morning weekday broadcasts of the winter Olympics.*

When I got the call, I cannot say that a divine light shone down or that I had some epiphany, but I did feel an obligation to help since nobody else was going to assist her. I decided to fly back to Stevens Point from Denver, move her home from the hospital, and get her set up for her extended recovery.

I remember the mother of my best friend from high school, who still lived in Stevens Point, picking me up from the airport. The look of sadness in her eyes as she plucked me from the frozen curb outside the airport remains with me to this day. I am not sure if she was sad that I felt I had to make the trip, or if she was sad for my mother because the only person who had come to help her was someone who so clearly did not want to be there. Maybe she felt it was okay now to let me know that she understood the train wreck that was my family.

Shortly after I arrived I jumped into action. I had a long to-do list and a short time to get everything done, which was probably a blessing; I could focus on immediate objectives and not dwell on the emotional aspect of being back in Stevens Point and around my mother. I hoped to be able to stay within my disconnected comfort zone.

Over the next few days my mother and I spent more time alone together than I think we had collectively over my entire life. Getting anything done was tough because my mom was obstinate and knew better than anyone else on every topic. We engaged in a curious mix of venting and educating. The pinnacle was when I was trying to get her a cell phone (her first).

Her strong desire for a universal communication device coupled with her lack of knowledge about what such a device could do was a challenge in itself. To add to the confusion, I was explaining her options over the phone while talking to a salesperson at the AT&T store. Had it not been so painful, it would have been comedic gold.

During one conversation, I did let her know that, given the history of our family and my place in it, I found it difficult to be warm and caring toward her. She did not take the bait to ask for more details, so I avoided getting into the abuse issues with my father and any particulars about my experiences with her. (This visit was before I had begun my deep dive into my personal emotional recovery or really opened up to anyone about my state of existence.) But my mother did nod and turn away in what I interpreted as embarrassment or maybe even shame.

I think that is when I realized my mother was human. Granted, she was highly flawed and could still demoralize me with a word or two, but I realized that she had struggled during my childhood, too, and that she did not receive the support she needed at that time. Yes, she was a bad actor. She neglected her children and was emotionally abusive. Nonetheless, she was human. I never had a moment like that with my father.

Better Grandmother Than Mother

After my son was born in the fall of 2002, my mom came to visit us in Colorado several times before her death from lung cancer in 2010. My mother's relationship with my young son was both heartbreaking and joyous to me. She would get down on the floor with him and make buildings with giant Duplo squares. I remember eavesdropping on them when they were dyeing Easter eggs one year, just to try and get a glimpse into her tender relationship with him.

She spoke gently and kindly to him and encouraged his efforts. I was elated that my son had a genuine connection with a grandparent, but it also broke my heart that I had never experienced this parent when I was a child. My initial reaction was not a healthy one: losing all perspective, I thought, *What was wrong with me that all you did was spew hatred when I was kid?* It is not a good place when you are jealous of your own child.

After some challenging reflection, I was able to embrace the fact that my mother actually had grown and changed after the divorce. I think she was able to become more of the person she wanted to be when I was child.

Even though our cordial exchanges never blossomed into a beautiful mother-son relationship, after spending time with us she would often send a thoughtful note expressing authentic emotion. It was as though she found it impossible to share her emotions with me in person, but she was able to write her feelings down and send them to me later. I knew she was really trying. Even though her efforts may have been a bit clumsy, she genuinely wanted to make a connection. I was finally able to see my mother as an actual flesh and blood person. She had not been a good mother; she hurt me and damaged me. But she did not break me.

I realized that she, too, was not entirely broken. She had created a new satisfying life for herself in Florida, filled with rescuing turtles, church involvement, and volunteering at the local art museum. I think she made some actual friends there before she died and was more a part of her community in Florida than she had ever been in Stevens Point. I continue to struggle to find a warm memory of my childhood with her, but unlike my father, my mother was eventually able to take some responsibility for creating the toxic environment in our household.

I was finally able to see my mother as an actual flesh and blood person. She had not been a good mother; she hurt me and damaged me. But she did not break me.

Though we never had a close relationship, she did show me that it is possible to change and become a better person for yourself and others, although she never would truly attempt to make amends or be directly accountable. Even when I revealed to her near the end of her life the abuse from my father, she was unable to do more than state that she never knew and provide a half-hearted, "I'm sorry," over the telephone.

FEAR DYNAMICS TECHNIQUE #5

CREATE A DECISION TREE

After the Fear Dynamics Technique of building in a pause became more natural to me, I realized I needed a larger framework to structure my thought process and actively use the pause. I wanted to be sure I was engaging in a rational process and not reacting solely on emotion. I was especially aware of, and concerned about, how the dynamics of fear were driving my choices, responses, and reactions and undermining my relationships. I needed a system to determine whether my fear and anxiety were rational or irrational—whether they were based on evidence, supposition, or historical reaction.

It was important to me during this phase of therapy to not only understand the origin of my issues, but to be able to incorporate this understanding into my daily life. I wanted to develop a personal system that could reliably frame my reaction to stimulus. I know this may sound overly scientific, but I needed a rational approach to replace my deeply ingrained irrational and often subconscious impulses.

As I have discussed, part of my mixed bag of psychological and emotional issues includes feeling as though people were attacking me whenever they asked a question or said anything to me or about me. Much of this stemmed from the relationship with my father, who I believe used every interaction with me as an opportunity to shame or belittle me to increase his sense of self-worth and exert his power at my expense.

> *It was important to me during this phase of therapy to not only understand the origin of my issues, but to be able to incorporate this understanding into my daily life.*

Growing up I was always on guard, and this profoundly affected how I related to people. Rarely did I see an interaction with someone as a neutral, non-aggressive encounter. I viewed virtually all conversation as a battle to avoid, win, or endure and—above all—escape. Once I had made progress in realizing that every interaction was not, in fact, an attack, I needed to devise a system to determine whether my perception of the situation was accurate. Was I really under attack? What evidence would support that conclusion? What motivation would this person have to attack me? What is really going on? These are the questions I needed to ask but was not asking or even thinking about before. Instead, I was hypersensitive and acting instinctively, impulsively. The fight, flight, or freeze response was dictating my thoughts and responses.

I developed an efficient technique to interrupt and assess my initial impulse so I could respond calmly and rationally in a meaningful and authentic way.

My Personal Decision Tree

The solution I came up with was to create my own personal decision tree. You don't have to be a math major (or even good at math) to understand the concept. You simply follow a trail of possible choices until you reach a decision, as shown below. This very basic decision tree reflects the thought process that goes into deciding what to order at a restaurant. First, the person decides whether to order from the breakfast or lunch menu. Then she chooses a category on the menu. Finally, she chooses an item from that category.

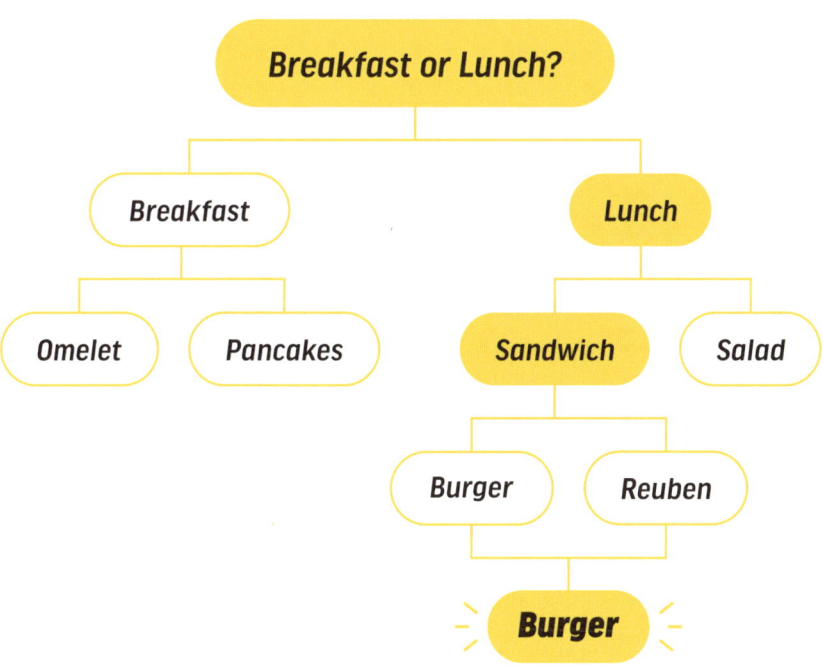

A basic decision tree.

Using a framework like the one described above, I designed a basic decision tree to help me evaluate my mental and emotional state as I interacted with people. This allowed me to think and respond more rationally to interactions. First, I ask myself: *Is this person asking me something that is objectively reasonable in this situation or behaving rationally given the actual context?* Meaning: if I step back and observe without me being the subject and pretend as if I am watching as a third party, is the other person behaving rationally? Based on that answer, I ask one of the following questions:

1. *If this person is engaging in a rational and reasonable manner, how do I want to respond?*

Or:

2. *If the person is not reasonable or rational, what do I need to do to engage and deal with that reality so I can proceed forward and not get sucked into their dynamic?*

This technique of asking a series of questions forces my mind to think more rationally and deliberately. It requires me to determine if I am the issue. I have to register what the person is saying, digest the words, put them in context, and then reflect on the person's intended meaning before delivering a genuine and thoughtful response. If, upon considering the question objectively, I determine most people would think it was a reasonable request, I internalize that the person was not creating the anxiety, that the anxiety was manifesting from within me, and that the other person has nothing to do with it. I make a mental note that I need to look at the personal issue later. After determining that the question is not an attack, I have freed myself to engage thoughtfully in the conversation.

When my anxiety level starts to rise, I ask myself a third question:

3. *Why am I feeling what I'm feeling?*

If I can deduce that the other person is being rational, I work hard to slow down my mind, focus on the conversation, and participate with clarity and confidence. I stow my anxiety to be unpacked at a later time. The issue with anxiety is that it has no sense of time. I may become anxious in a conversation because my mind is triggered by something the person said that subconsciously reminds my brain of an event or conversation from my childhood. Unbeknownst to the person I am talking to, I have just been sent back forty years to Plover, Wisconsin, where I lived in an almost constant state of agitation.

In the past, I would have disconnected from this conversation and retreated into my own shell, at best. At worst, I may have been dismissive or even rude to that person. I can see now how, in those situations, the other person did not deserve that treatment. Definitely fear dynamics in action. By working through and examining the origin of my feelings of anxiety, I can stay in the present and realize that I am safe and in control of myself in this interaction. I can engage to achieve goals and be proactive rather than reactive and agitated. Using a decision tree that's informed by the dynamics of fear has helped me immeasurably in relating to others, in both professional and personal relationships, in an honest and authentic way.

> *By working through and examining the origin of my feelings of anxiety, I can stay in the present and realize that I am safe and in control of myself in this interaction.*

You Don't Need to Know Everything or Solve Every Problem

In my professional life as an attorney, I work on big, complex deals involving people buying and selling companies or creating business relationships. Many times, tensions run high because much is at stake and people always want to get the deal done as quickly as possible. Building in a pause and using my decision tree have enabled me to interact with sincerity, collaborate with others, and act without fear of engaging in or being confronted by the process. It takes time, effort, and constant vigilance, but I can see the dividends in professional success and overall personal happiness, as well as in stronger connections with clients and colleagues.

Earlier in my career, I assumed clients would expect me to know everything and be able to answer every question off the top of my head. I now recognize the absurdity of that assumption, but back then when I didn't know an answer, I wouldn't admit it and I would blame others and then punish myself to try and find a solution in an unreasonable timeframe. Now, without hesitation, I'll say, "I don't understand what you just said. Can you explain that to me?" There was a time in my life when I never thought I'd be so candid with anyone, let alone a business partner or client.

Taking time to analyze a situation has also enabled me to identify the fear dynamics of the situation. Other people's emotional issues might affect their decisions or influence the thoughts, emotions, and behaviors of other participants.

> **Pro Tip:** Acknowledging that an issue is not a "money issue" or a "legal issue" but an "emotional issue" often helps to resolve deal points much more efficiently.

I have found that just stating that there may be some fear dynamics going on and it's more than a clear business issue has helped many clients pause on their own and think about the broader context and possible solutions that may never have occurred to them before.

Take Your Time: It Is a Process

This technique of creating a decision tree and learning to use it is a process. Do not expect smooth sailing the first (or hundredth) time you apply it. When I started to implement this technique, there were times I would only go through the decision tree days after the actual interaction because it was just too much to do in real time. I kept working on it and after a while, it did become second nature. I can now go through my decision tree so quickly that the process is imperceptible to others, often during the pause I have created.

> *Earlier in my career, when I didn't know an answer, I wouldn't admit it. Now, without hesitation, I'll say, "I don't understand what you just said. Can you explain that to me?"*

For example, in the past, if opposing legal counsel was in full-on tantrum mode complete with proverbial throwing of papers and "stomping out of the room" (believe me, it happens more than you think), I would get very anxious, shut down, disconnect, and blame myself for the situation. Unfortunately, that fear-based response was counterproductive to resolving whatever issue led to the outburst, and it was not effective for serving my clients.

Now, using my decision tree, I can objectively size up the situation very quickly, conclude that opposing counsel is behaving irrationally, and calmly and intelligently engage with everyone involved to come up with a mutually beneficial solution. The beauty of this is that I do not need to figure out what the other person's issue is, just that it is not my issue. As a result, I can then focus on solutions and not add to the mayhem. (Of course, if this interaction is with a loved one, you may want to discuss later any underlying issues that may have caused the outburst.)

That being said, the decision tree has often revealed situations in which my thoughts or actions were misguided and tangled up with reactions driven by my past, especially when I first started using it. Whenever this occurs, I note it and reflect on it later to improve my future performance and thinking.

Empowering Yourself with Careful Deliberation

These techniques of slowing down, building in a pause, and using your personal decision tree will empower you in any setting— at work, at home, or even in casual encounters outside those two environments. While employing this system, you can be confident that you are engaging with the world rationally, with careful deliberation, and not from a place of fear or anxiety or misunderstood reactivity.

In the workplace, a forthright yet thoughtful response gains you respect. People will seek you out, not only for your knowledge and expertise, but also for your wisdom and your ability to lead people in resolving conflict and working to find solutions.

In your personal relationships, a thoughtful response demonstrates that you heard and understood what the other person had to say, and you took their opinion, perspective, and the information they provided into careful consideration before formulating your response. It will help to prevent you from feeling as though you are always being attacked, ignored, or marginalized, because you will gain more control over yourself and your interactions with others.

In casual encounters outside your professional and personal circles, nobody will be able to "push your buttons" or "ruffle your feathers." You will put their words and actions in the proper perspective, avoid the negative dynamics of fear that tend to get in your way, and respond accordingly by pausing to develop an appropriate response. Everyone will be better off in these situations.

> *Slowing down, building in a pause, and using your personal decision tree will empower you in any setting.*

Remember, you will never live the life you want if you suffer constantly from undifferentiated anxiety. Sadly, you may not even be able to figure out what you want in life because your entire being is so emotionally overstimulated and preoccupied that no space remains for you to be present and to rationally examine what you want and need to be happy.

I know this because I lived it. For years the simplest conversations left me feeling attacked and anxious, and I would have no way of knowing why I felt that way or even what I was feeling. Part of what helped me was slowing my brain down during interactions with others. Pausing, taking a breath, and checking in with my little guy all helped me enormously. Slowing down ultimately led me to understand the root of my anxiety in the situation. It works to build in a pause and use your personal decision tree.

Think to yourself: *Is what the person said objective and reasonable for this situation?* If it is, take a deep breath, let your anxiety dissipate, and engage with calmness and clarity. In the beginning, this process could take fifteen minutes, an hour, or longer. At first, you may even engage in the process several days after the interaction. Over time, and with plenty of practice, you will be able to use this technique to conduct your analysis quickly and almost effortlessly.

Success begins with practice.

Success begins with practice. What begins as a tiny habit grows into a standard operating procedure in your life until you finally notice how fundamentally different you are from the anxious person you used to be. I use these tools every day at work, at home, and when I am out and about. I rely on them. Now when I wake up in the morning, my mind is relaxed, and my heart is open.

Chapter 4
LIFE GOES ON

After high school, I attended the University of Minnesota, Minneapolis. I didn't have any big career goals when I started college. I did not, for example, dream of being a lawyer at the time. I was relieved to be out of the house. All I wanted to do was get good grades and a college diploma.

Soon after moving to campus, I visited my older sister who attended the same university, but lived off campus. She had been asking me to visit her more, which I found strange at the time because it wasn't like we ever had any real relationship when we were growing up.

Our family was more akin to five strangers living under one roof and sharing meals and holidays together. It wasn't what I imagined a real family to be, or what I saw on TV or read about in books.

In retrospect, I think my sister was trying to be a good sister and look out for me, and I was just too damaged and disconnected to be able to genuinely engage with her.

Gradually, I started to become more "myself" in college and made some true friends, but I still was tethered to my parents and visited them on major holidays, which soon became more complicated.

A Perfect Opportunity for Divorce

During my freshmen year of college, my parents divorced. Immediately afterward they petitioned the church to annul their marriage of more than twenty years (despite having three children). I don't fully understand the laws of the Catholic Church on this issue, but the church granted this annulment, which freed my father to remarry a few years later in a church wedding. Given the difficulty of getting an annulment instead of "just" a divorce, I felt as though our parents were trying to officially erase my existence and that of my siblings.

After the divorce, my brother, who was still in high school, chose to live with my dad in Boston. My dad had done a remarkable job of convincing most people that Mom was the problem, so I was not shocked by my brother's choice. I never fully bought into my dad's misrepresentations about his paternal superiority, but my brother definitely believed that narrative at that time. Maybe it was because my brother seemingly had a more normal relationship with our dad than I did. From what I know, my dad never asked my brother to go for late-night swims in the river or get him alone to watch a movie in the basement. Back then, when my brother lived with my dad, I never talked to him about how Dad abused me. I was too ashamed and was afraid he wouldn't believe me.

Mom tried to connect with me during the end of my college career. I think being divorced from my dad was a positive step for her own personal development. I remember she drove to Minneapolis from Stevens Point to attend the ceremony when I was admitted to Phi Beta Kappa my junior year. But I also recall her clear disappointment when I told her I was going to Georgetown Law School in Washington, D.C., and did not get into Harvard.

The Law School Years

Law school was a time of growth for me. The first year of law school seems designed to be exceedingly difficult. Success requires singular focus and often social deprivation. Right up my alley. During my second year of law school, I made unconscious strides to become more *me*. Living fully on my own and distancing myself from my family allowed me to stumble out of my complete disconnection. For the first time, I started making decisions based on what I liked and what I wanted to do. I started to think that maybe I did matter in this world.

During my first year at Georgetown, I made a good friend, Jason, and we roomed together my second and third year of law school. He really helped me become more social and more connected with the world around me. Around this time, I was also starting to stand up to my parents. As I related earlier, my mother sent me a care package that I promptly returned unopened. This act of rebellion shocked Jason, who perceived it as cruel, but it was a big step forward for me. My skin seemed to be mine for the first time, and I felt that I could look forward with some hope. Distancing from my family diluted its toxicity. I was forming authentic friendships with others and felt confident that I was going to be successful in life.

My third year of law school began as the best in my life so far.

I had a job offer waiting for me when I graduated, I had a group of friends, and I had a serious girlfriend whom I was planning to marry the summer after graduation. Emotionally, I was in the best place I had ever been. In retrospect, I had a long way to go.

My fiancée knew I had a fractured relationship with my mother because I was keenly in touch with that anger at the time, but she knew nothing of the secret past I had with my father. To her, he was the good parent. I felt as though I had emerged from the storm of my childhood and that nothing more needed to be done. I imagined working in downtown Minneapolis and eventually owning a home. My dark past was fading in the rearview mirror and I was driving down the road toward a brighter future.

Mugged

Then, fate intervened, and all the progress I managed to make unconsciously on my own was seemingly wiped away. It was a typical early spring Friday evening in D.C., although I do remember it being unseasonably warm that night. I was walking to my fiancée's apartment in the Adams Morgan area after an afternoon of studying and meetings with the financial aid department at Georgetown Law to go over my student loans. I was in the middle of a tree-lined city block of apartments with cars parked on both sides of the street. Streetlights were on and a woman on the other side of the street was walking in the opposite direction. Three young men walked past me.

As I started to take my next step, I felt my duffle bag being ripped from me. This duffle bag was my life. It contained my glasses, my books, my notes and outlines for studying, and, most important, all my law school student loan papers. This was before everything was online, so hard copies of documents were sometimes the only copy of documents that existed.

> *Then, fate intervened, and all the progress I managed to make unconsciously on my own was seemingly wiped away.*

I grabbed the shoulder strap instinctively. I was not going to let go. I had worked too hard for everything inside it. They were irreplaceable items to me, but of no value to anyone else. My efforts seemed to only make these guys more determined. They pushed and shoved me and tried to get the bag, but they couldn't pry my grip from it. They upped their efforts with a baseball bat and hit me several times across my back and legs. I fell to the ground, still clutching my bag, but I knew I had lost. One man ripped the bag from me while another kicked me and the third rifled through the pockets in my jeans and took my money clip (all of fifteen dollars, my driver's license, credit card, and a subway pass). As I lay on the ground, all I could think was, *Why?*

A short time later, a police car and ambulance arrived. Someone must have called 911. I was badly bruised, but the EMT said no bones were broken, and I had not hit my head so I didn't need to go to the hospital. The police took a statement and told me they did not have any real hope of finding the men or my belongings.

After I had spent about a half hour with the EMT and police, my fiancée arrived and drove me back to her apartment. I canceled my credit card and requested a replacement, got new glasses at Tysons Corner mall the next day, and on Monday, went to the

DMV to get a new driver's license and made an appointment with the student loan office to begin the bureaucratic nightmare of recreating all my loan history.

I handled my assault practically and unemotionally. I didn't discuss it with my fiancée or my friend Jason, despite their urging. The school suggested I talk to a therapist, so I did—twice. I didn't need to talk about it. I didn't pause to feel angry, victimized, or sad, or to feel any emotion at all. This was just something that happened in the world. My childhood had provided excellent training on how to survive an unwarranted attack—pretend it did not affect you.

When I look back at this event now, I can see clearly that I had immediately reverted to my core survival mode and foundational belief that nobody was there for me, the world was against me, and I did not deserve any happiness. I regressed to the emotionless, disconnected version of myself that had finally started to fade into the background. I had completely discounted the mugging as inconsequential.

If any one of my friends had been attacked, I would have been aghast at what a traumatic ordeal they had survived. But because it was me, who did not matter, I acted as though it was no big deal. If I hadn't been mugged or had responded to it in a healthier way, maybe I would have been able to continue on the more connected trajectory I had started to establish in law school. But that mugging marked the day I turned autopilot back on and stepped back onto the moving walkway.

Life After Law School

A few weeks after the attack, I graduated from law school, moved to Minneapolis, took the bar exam, started a new job, and got married—just a few huge life changes after surviving a major trauma, right? Definitely the right move on my part, I can now say with sarcasm. In all honesty, it never dawned on me to reconsider or postpone my plans. I have no idea what may have happened had I not been attacked. Would I have recognized that I wasn't at all prepared for marriage and that I didn't really know my fiancée (let alone myself) very well? Would I have realized that maybe I was getting married because it was the next logical step after graduating law school and because I was afraid to face the future alone?

As I started my professional life in Minneapolis, my life continued on a stable path. Was I happy? I thought so at the time, but in hindsight, not in any meaningful way. Did I feel connected to my life? No. Frankly, I didn't even feel connected to myself. Did I care? Not really. I was rising in the ranks at my job and making a respectable income. My wife had a good job, too. We were in the process of buying a home in a solid neighborhood. My wife and I didn't fight. Our household was calm, dependable, and predictable. I had the life I thought I wanted. I thought this must be what it felt like to be a contented adult. Trouble is, it wasn't.

> *True change does not and cannot happen by chance or luck; it requires deliberate effort.*

Looking back at this time of my life revealed to me a profound insight: True change does not and cannot happen by chance or luck; it requires deliberate effort. I deeply believe that if I would have had professional help at this time, or if someone had compelled me to examine myself, or if I had been further along in my own emotional development, I may have taken a different path. Or, I would have taken the same path, making the same choices, but with greater deliberation, conscious intent, and the involvement of people close to me.

Instead, I disconnected from myself to avoid engaging the fears and anxiety surrounding these decisions and therefore do not believe I made deliberate and thoughtful choices about the life I wanted.

Chapter 5

MEETING MRS. RIGHT WHEN I WAS MR. WRONG

We've all had pivotal moments in our lives, turning points that caused a major shift in the direction we were traveling on our journeys of becoming. You may not even realize at the time that these moments would be game changers, but you look back on your life with some perspective and they stand out with the utmost clarity. I have experienced two such moments in my life.

By the spring of 1997, I was pretty much numb emotionally. I wasn't unhappy but definitely wasn't happy either. Objectively, I felt that I should be satisfied with my life. I was married and I had a good job. In my mind at that time, what else was there? I felt no reason to change my life in any drastic way. Maybe I thought about trying to eat healthier, but I was not contemplating any massive life change like the encounter that blew up my life in May of 1997.

On May 6, I met the woman who would become my second wife and, I hope, my intimate companion for the rest of my life. We met during a corporate retreat for our law firm at a quaint resort on one of Minnesota's 10,000 lakes. She worked in the Denver office and I worked in the Minneapolis office. At the retreat, an all-hands meeting of attorneys was about to start after the usual social proceedings of the day. For me that meant I had just finished golfing with some colleagues.

I walked in, dreading the upcoming corporate speak, and I saw her sitting alone in the back row of the conference room. Inexplicably, I was drawn to her. I immediately headed to the back row, sat next to her, and struck up a conversation. I can't recall what I said (I'm sure it was inane) or what she said, but I didn't want to stop talking to her, even when the speaker—the managing partner of the firm—began his presentation.

As the presentation commenced, I sat in silence next to her in a room full of other attorneys, trying to figure out what was happening to me. I was having trouble thinking clearly, and I felt an actual electric charge course through my body, but I had no insight into, or understanding of, what was taking shape inside me. At the end of the presentation, she stood up and wandered off to catch up with other associates. *What a relief!* I thought to myself, *Okay, good, she's gone.*

After a plated dinner that evening, everyone gathered in the backwoods-themed bar at the resort. I specifically wanted to avoid talking to this attorney from Denver, but when I found myself in a group of associates, she was the only one I found interesting.

I soon reached the conclusion that I did not really want to avoid her. Before I knew it, four hours had gone by with us talking, laughing, and playing a Mortal Kombat video game.

> *I felt an immediate emotional connection,*
> *different from anything prior in my life.*

As we continued to talk, I let her know I was married and was seemingly lost in the relationship, which translated to being unhappy. We were both originally from Wisconsin, so we shared stories about growing up as "cheeseheads." I told her superficially about my dysfunctional family and alluded to alcohol being a factor. We also talked about our fears and frustrations with being young lawyers.

To this day, I am not sure why I opened up to this person, but the words just tumbled out. I resonated with this woman on a deeper level than with anyone I had ever met. She sparked something in me, and for the first time, I felt an immediate emotional connection, different from anything prior in my life. Time seemed to stand still, but clearly it hadn't because suddenly no one else was there and the bartender informed us we needed to leave.

I walked her back to her cottage and kissed her. Although I was certainly confused and unhappy with my current life, I had never cheated on my wife. What was I doing? I was simultaneously elated and horribly confused. When I was with this woman, I felt more engaged and vibrant than ever before. Yet I knew that my marriage was not awful, and my wife was not a bad person.

My wife certainly did not cause my anxiety in our marriage. It came from within me, from my disconnectedness and inability to know and be who I was.

Something about this woman from Denver pierced through the shell that protected me from my own emotions. Something about this interaction made me feel more whole and genuine. The harsh dilemma was that I cared for my wife and knew that she had done nothing to deserve the chaos that was about to take over my life, and therefore hers.

This woman from Denver woke the next morning and flew home, probably thinking she would never see me or talk to me again, fully prepared to move on with her life. As for me, I felt my life crashing down around me.

Instead, I returned home from the retreat and told my wife I wasn't sure I wanted to be married anymore—that I wasn't sure of anything anymore and needed to figure myself out. This sounds so clear and straightforward, but I was a complete wreck and felt as though every muscle in my body was cramping as I started the conversation. I didn't want to hurt her. I'm sure I caught her completely off guard but the discussion did not snowball into a big fight as I was afraid it might. When I stood there talking to her, part of me was stupefied at what I was doing, yet I knew somewhere deep inside that I had to be honest with her because something monumental had shifted inside of me.

I understand it seems inconsistent to feel that I needed to be honorable in telling my wife as quickly as I could what was happening even when I could not fully understand. Yet at the same time, I was instigating this chaos by my choices. Surprisingly, I was not disconnecting and avoiding. I was purposefully trying to engage and communicate my feelings, which was something entirely new for me to do. I chose a path that was true, despite the upheaval that was guaranteed to come.

My wife was shocked, but not reactive. I am not fully sure what she felt because I think my revelation came from nowhere, and in that instant, I suspect she suddenly doubted everything. Over the ensuing months, we tried to engage and talk about what was happening to our relationship and why. It was fits and starts with neither of us really knowing what to do, and not having any real guidance. Ultimately, after many painful months, we decided to separate, then divorce.

> *Surprisingly, I was not disconnecting and avoiding. I was purposefully trying to engage and communicate my feelings, which was something entirely new for me to do. I chose a path that was true, despite the upheaval that was guaranteed to come.*

Truth be told, I was in such a free fall and unable to act or even articulate what I was thinking or feeling that I believe she did not see a path forward and decided she could not live in that limbo. Once we decided to divorce, the process was amicable. Our conversations together as we went through the divorce process were actually some of the most thoughtful times we spent together. I think we both realized that while we cared for each other, we should never have gotten married.

After the initial conversation with my wife on that fateful

Sunday, I called information to get the phone number of Libby, the attorney from Denver who had unwittingly pierced my protective shield at the retreat in Minnesota. She had not arrived home from the retreat yet, so I left a message. I spoke to her the following day and we stayed in regular contact from that point on. We didn't go more than a few days at a time without communicating until I moved to Denver in August 1998.

As I reflect on this significant period in my life, I realize I had been disconnected emotionally from my wife long before that fateful weekend retreat and, up until that Sunday when we finally talked about it, I had been completely disconnected from my own emotions. In the days following this conversation, I honestly think I had a bit of a nervous breakdown. My head and emotions were swirling and I was physically uncomfortable in my skin. I felt as though my brain and body were wrapped in sandpaper. The irritation and discomfort were nearly constant, and every movement mentally or physically agitated me.

Fortunately, I realized I needed professional help and I soon found a good therapist and started seeing her twice a week. She was able to help me calm down and start sorting out my thoughts and emotions. I had never been to any sort of therapist on a regular basis before. The sessions were incredibly helpful, enabling me to regain my composure and start to scratch the surface of my emotions and needs.

My therapist introduced me to a psychotherapy called Eye Movement Desensitization and Reprocessing (EMDR), which was developed to alleviate the distress associated with traumatic memories. During therapy we would discuss emotionally disturbing issues or events while I focused on light motion controlled by the therapist. The goal of this therapy was to enable me to access and process some traumatic memories with my therapist. During this process I could feel the depth of the emotion attached to the memories without shutting down or disconnecting. This allowed me to experience the emotions and understand that they were now just memories and that they would not destroy me.

As soon as I was no longer terrified of the memories, I could sort them out, dig in, and develop an understanding and appreciation for what they triggered in me as an adult. This understanding allowed me to create new mental/emotional associations between the traumatic memories and how to deal with their effect on me in the present. In short, EMDR enabled me to reprogram the pathways of fear and terror associated with certain memories so that I did not become derailed by them. I could now use them to create productive and positive insight to my current life. Through these EMDR sessions I was trying to connect with, and work through, many of the emotions I had suppressed from years of my father's abuse and mother's neglect.

> *This allowed me to experience the emotions and understand that they were now just memories and that they would not destroy me.*

This process helped me speak about these issues while being emotionally connected. A great first step. I started to be able to right my sinking ship, get a handle on my feelings, and make it through each day with purpose, as opposed to being a naked nerve twitching at the most minimal perceived provocation or unexpected event.

I shared what I was going through with a couple of my lifelong and most trusted friends. I'm not sure they fully understood, but they listened and engaged with me as I told them what was going on. I was divorced some months later. My therapist and friends all advised me not to even think about starting a relationship with this attorney in Denver and that I needed to focus on myself and getting emotionally healthy. I knew that was the prudent thing to do and wanted to heed that advice. But, of course, I chose not to.

Libby and I continued our long-distance relationship. After a year, I decided to move to Denver because I felt Minneapolis was just not a place I wanted to be, and I wanted to dive in and see if a day-to-day relationship with Libby could be real. Once I settled into Denver, I found another good therapist and continued my work with him. He was very helpful in getting me to really dig into the facts, chronology, and reality of the abuse with my father and move toward accepting that reality.

As I look back on it, my therapist in Minneapolis was really performing triage work with me. She did not have the time to spend with me that was needed, and I was unable to really dig deeply into the myriad issues. In hindsight, I stopped short with both therapists before doing the hard work of integrating my history into my present life to realize how it still affected me. I thought it was enough to admit and acknowledge the facts and make the superficial connections, then forget them and move forward. I would later learn that more difficult work was required.

> *I started to be able to right my sinking ship, get a handle on my feelings, and make it through each day with purpose, as opposed to being a naked nerve twitching at the most minimal perceived provocation or unexpected event.*

Libby and I continued our relationship but did not move in together. After a couple of years, she reasonably wanted to get married. I didn't want the relationship to end and I loved her, but I continued to disconnect and pushed her away. I was afraid, and I was not going to get married again until I felt I was ready. In my first marriage I had hurt someone I deeply cared for, and I was not going to risk doing that again.

I think my fear of another possible broken relationship made me retreat, and part of me just wanted Libby to make the decision to leave and save me the pain of actually doing it myself. But a bigger part of me wanted her in my life and I could catch a glimpse of what could become a happy life. So, we went to couples counseling. I wanted her to know I was working hard to get where she wanted me to be and where I needed to be before I would feel comfortable moving forward.

I still cannot fathom why Libby stayed. I was such an ass at times: sullen, reserved, and uncommunicative. Little did I realize I was as important to her as she was to me. It took a long time and many frustrating conversations for me to finally believe that she loved me . . . that I was somehow capable of being loved. I finally came to accept that I was not a pawn in some elaborate scheme the universe was plotting to humiliate me. I was able to trust myself and accept the happiness I felt when I was with Libby. We married in a small mountainside cabin in Beaver Creek, Colorado, in late September 2001 on a radiant fall mountain day. A little more than a year later, we welcomed our beautiful son, Nicholas. A happy family . . .

Libby, baby Nicholas, and me, 2003.

GET OFF AUTOPILOT

I realized that I spent huge portions of my life on autopilot. I made big decisions—going to law school, getting married for the first time—without being emotionally connected to the results of my choices. It seemed as though I was following a prescribed, well-known path to success and happiness.

We all engage in subconscious actions and decisions in our daily life to some degree. Have you ever driven home from work and not remembered anything about your trip home? Or maybe you attended a pitch meeting at work that left you wondering whether you had participated? Or maybe, more significantly, after leaving your child's bedroom at night, you cannot recall a single word your four-year-old son told you before going to sleep?

I call this "living life on autopilot," and it is pretty much how I lived the better part of my first thirty-seven years. I was doing everything associated with living but I wasn't living my life with conscious intent or direction. After I recognized I was living on autopilot, figuring out how to get off of it and stay off of it became a significant goal of my therapy.

Don't get me wrong—autopilot is great for routine flying in clear skies with little to no turbulence when the plane is already airborne. It's not so great for taxiing to or from runways, handling take-offs and landings, making corrections when wayward birds fly into the engines, or responding to other unexpected conditions or events. In situations such as those, the best pilot is a well-trained human who is alert, present, and focused.

Likewise, personal autopilot is okay when you are driving a route you have driven thousands of times before or wheeling your cart around a familiar grocery store to pick up a few items for dinner. It keeps us fresh for the moments when we need to be engaged. However, many of us switch to autopilot when we need to act amidst paralyzing fear or anxiety. Autopilot enables us to continue outwardly functioning while remaining mentally and emotionally detached. It is a great self-defense mechanism for maintaining stability, but while autopilot is engaged we are not truly living, adapting, growing, loving, or actually engaging with anyone. I know because this is how I lived for many years.

If autopilot describes how you are living your life most of the time, I suggest you consider another approach—another way of living in which you are more present and connected to yourself and others throughout the day. Try turning off your autopilot.

Symptoms of a Life Lived on Autopilot

A life lived on autopilot is like a hollow tree: it looks fine on the outside, but is empty on the inside. From a distance nobody can tell it is sick and weak, vulnerable to crashing down, burning up, or rotting out. Like us, the tree began its life as a hearty organism, full of life. Then, something happened to stress the tree—maybe too much or too little water, weather that was too hot or too cold, or physical damage to its roots or bark. In a weakened state the tree becomes more susceptible to other threats such as pests or fungi that eat the tree from the inside out. In this state the tree is still a tree, but a shell of its former self.

> *A life lived on autopilot is like a hollow tree: it looks fine on the outside, but is empty on the inside.*

A similar scenario can unfold if you suffer mental or emotional trauma. The traumatic event or ongoing circumstances can trigger a chain reaction that leads to a downward spiral. It may begin with a sense of shame, guilt, or disillusionment, leading to a loss of self-worth that makes you withdraw from the world to avoid the pain. You sink into yourself, seldom expressing your thoughts and feelings except in the form of chronic despair or bouts of sudden rage when you're overwhelmed by anxiety, fear, or frustration. You become so defensive that nothing can penetrate your outer shell to nourish your growth and development, and you become an empty husk of yourself.

Perhaps you or someone you know can identify with this dynamic. Maybe you actively avoid the "stop and chat" at work because your heart races and fear floods your system when someone comes up to you and says hello. Maybe you stay home from family weddings, graduations, or funerals because you don't want to be forced to interact with others. Maybe your list of real-life friends—not social media friends—has dwindled to a precious one or two people because everyone else makes you uncomfortable. As life passes you by, you become more brittle and less resilient, like the hollowed-out tree. More and more of your day is spent on autopilot to escape this fear and anxiety without you even realizing that you have disconnected.

Fear Dynamics

Anxiety and fear kill personal and professional relationships. They end marriages and careers and suffocate goals and dreams. I know firsthand about this destructive power because this dynamic duo almost destroyed my life until I realized I needed to tackle my personal issues and understand the dynamics of fear—the patterns of communication and reaction that emerge during personal interactions when any one or more parties involved is feeling afraid or anxious.

Here's an example of fear dynamics in the workplace: I was working with an accounting group on an acquisition for a client and one of the CPAs assisting on the deal was constantly offering advice—some of it outside his area of expertise—and putting forth a great effort to drive the transaction forward. His behavior seemed as peculiar as it was annoying, until I discovered that he was up for a promotion to partner. His fear of not making partner was making him overreach in our joint representation.

Once I learned of the impending promotion and realized that a fear dynamic had developed, I stressed to him that our client valued consensus among professionals and a sense that all of us were working in concert to achieve the client's objectives. After raising the issue and trying to focus on a common goal, the CPA and I were able to coordinate our efforts. He was allowed to do what he did best without feeling left out or thinking he needed to impress his firm's leadership.

The CPA was elevated to partner later that year and our client complimented both of our firms on how well we worked together—two great results that may not have occurred without recognizing the fear and related anxiety creeping into the interactions.

Turning Off Autopilot

Over the course of my childhood I developed deep-seated anxiety, fear, and distrust, which I continued to have trouble dealing with for my entire life. These emotions were baked into my autopilot, causing me to universally disconnect from myself, as well as the people around me. As I became more aware of fear dynamics and the harm they can cause, I realized that I had to force myself off autopilot. This was no small feat because the fear of losing that self-defense mechanism I had relied on my entire life was overwhelming.

While life was not great for me, it also, objectively, was pretty darn good. Would people like the real me? Who was the real me? Would I still be able to practice law? In addition, autopilot had become a deeply entrenched habit. What drove me to make the leap, to force myself off autopilot, was the realization that the people in my life were worth the effort and, more important, that I was worth the effort.

> As I became more aware of fear dynamics and the harm they can cause, I realized that I had to force myself off autopilot.

People from all walks of life suffer from fear and anxiety. Anxiety is an equal-opportunity destroyer. It attacks people across the globe from every economic background, race, religion, gender orientation, body type, and age group. Sadly, many children as young as five report symptoms of chronic anxiety. Or worse, they disconnect from the world to avoid anger, sadness, and other strong feelings because they do not have a system to help them cope. Also, sadly, they never say a word to anyone. These children grow into adults who struggle with fear and anxiety on an ongoing basis but have learned to repress their feelings with highly developed autopilots.

Autopilot protects the fearful and the anxious, and people convince themselves that it hides them from detection from the outside world, even loved ones, enabling them to fly under the radar. Many adults move through life and by all appearances are successful and happy people while struggling internally with fear and anxiety and are profoundly unhappy.

Because you are reading this book, I suspect you probably recognize some degree of anxiety-driven autopilot or avoidance at work and in your personal life. Maybe you skip answering certain phone calls or take the least-traveled path out of the office to evade colleagues. At times, you may even dread leaving your home, and you make excuses to bow out of social commitments. You may be the person everyone thinks is living the dream, while deep down inside, you know better. You are engaged in a persistent struggle against the fear that you are about to fail at your job, as a parent, or as a friend, and have your true self (which you have convinced yourself is useless) revealed.

Regardless of the source of any fear and anxiety you are feeling, you have probably coped with it as most people do, and as I had done—by shutting down the part of you that is your essence, the part of you that is required to establish genuine connections with others. How do you reconnect with the people who matter in your life? How do you reconnect with yourself? You do so by turning off autopilot and reclaiming control of your life.

Turning off autopilot requires a conscious effort. You need to get out of your head and engage with others and with the world around you. This is not a self-study exercise; you will need to engage others. Below are the four steps to the Fear Dynamics Technique of getting off autopilot. This is a framework for you to follow to try and engage with your world on a moment-to-moment basis.

> *You may be the person everyone thinks is living the dream, while deep down inside, you know better.*

Step 1: *Look around*

The first step is to **look around**. People who experience fear and anxiety tend to be laser-focused when carrying out their daily tasks. They not only overlook the big picture, but they miss out on most everything else in the world. It is like vacationers sitting on the beach fixated on their phones in the middle of paradise. If they would just take the time to look around, to interact with others, to wander out into the water and maybe peek beneath the surface, imagine the richness of their experience.

The next time you go to the grocery store look around, wander all the aisles to see what you may be missing. Observe people and genuinely engage with them. For instance, ask the deli clerk how his day is going. Chances are good he will be shocked that you honored his existence.

> *Turning off autopilot requires a conscious effort. You need to get out of your head and engage with others and with the world around you.*

Step 2: *Look people in the eye*

Second, **look people in the eye**. I know we've talked about this already but it is essential to getting off autopilot. Looking people in the eye means everyone —loved ones, colleagues, casual friends, and strangers. Connecting through eye contact is one of the most important ways to engage with the world and connect with others. It can feel scary and it makes you vulnerable, but it is well worth the risk. Generally, people will respond favorably.

Step 3: *Listen to and register what people say*

Third, **listen to and register what people say.** How many times have you asked someone their name, only to forget it immediately upon hearing it? It used to happen to me all the time. When I am anxious my mind races, my thoughts get jumbled, and I start thinking about the other person's expectations of me, what I need or want to say next, or what—if anything—I am getting out of the interaction. I hear what the person says, but my brain does not process it. Almost immediately, I get so spun up inside it is as though the person were whispering from across the room. My inner thoughts are so cacophonous I fully expect the other person to interrupt by politely asking, "Could your neurotic thoughts please be a little quieter?"

Pro Tip: To remain present and connected, slow down your mind and remain fully in the moment.

Empty your mind of all other thoughts, past and present, and focus on understanding what the other person is saying as if your life depends on describing the discussion to someone else later. It is all about being in the moment and staying in the present.

Step 4: Ask questions and really listen to the answers

This leads me to the fourth action item to turn off autopilot: **Ask questions and really listen to the answers.** Remember that scenario of putting your child to bed and not remembering what you talked about? I bet if you would have asked your child questions and listened attentively to the answers, you would have stayed in the moment and remembered the conversation, and your child would have felt a closer connection to you. Same goes for an office meeting. If you ask questions with the conscious intent of fully understanding what others are trying to convey, your mind and emotions will be present during the meeting and you'll stay connected—your mind will be less apt to wander. I'm not suggesting you ask stupid, meaningless questions, rather that you actually engage with people and ask questions that amplify your understanding and deepen your connection. If you have accomplished the third action item of listening to what people say, this fourth step will be a breeze.

That's it; four steps and you are well on your way to disengaging autopilot, managing fear dynamics, and actively engaging with the people and the world around you. Master these steps and the fear and anxiety you feel will begin to dissipate as you get out of your head, become actively engaged in facing your fear, and discover that life is not so scary after all. In addition, as a reward for your efforts, you will begin to have richer and more meaningful experiences and interactions. You will begin to actively live your life instead of being moved passively along in whatever direction your circumstances dictate.

> *Four steps and you are well on your way to disengaging autopilot, managing the dynamics of fear, and actively engaging with the people and the world around you.*

When I shifted my perspective to conscious intent, it made me feel more connected not only to myself, but to the people around me. I fall back on this four-step Fear Dynamics Technique when I notice that I am anxious in a situation and it helps me re-engage and actively participate in the moment.

Chapter 6

THE CRASH AND BURN

Remember that lovely image of my wedding to Libby and the birth of our son. Wouldn't this picture be a beautiful finish to my story? I do so wish that this was the final scene in the romantic comedy version of my life, but—spoiler alert— it's not over, not by a long shot. There is significant heartache, confusion, and pain still to come before we get to the end of this story.

Recall my previous point about integration? Don't get me wrong, I had made massive progress during those five years before Libby and I married. It was significant that I was able to get married with clarity and confidence and the assurance that I had sufficient parenting skills to raise a child. Getting to this point was no small achievement and I felt confident I had whipped my demons and had it all figured out. I found truth in the cliché "pride goeth before the fall." So, after we were married, I stopped seeing my therapist and pretty much stopped actively looking inward or working on myself emotionally.

I had other responsibilities that moved to the front of the line now that I believed I had put my internal issues to rest—especially after Nick was born. I now had the fiscal responsibility of supporting three people, and I struggled deep down with professional insecurity. I wanted to focus more on my career and provide financial security for us. In fact, when our son was a toddler, I moved from a small law firm with a great culture to a larger firm to advance my career. I constantly battled the anxiety and fear that I was going to fail at my job, be revealed as a fraud, and be unable to provide for my family.

> *Looking back at it objectively, I can see that plenty of space was available had I just taken a more active role.*

The home front suffered from my anxieties and fears as well. Irrationally, I subconsciously began to resent Libby because she was so focused on our son. She was so wrapped up in issues such as choosing a preschool or taking Nick to classes or playdates with other kids that it seemed like little space was left in her heart or her life for me. Of course, looking back at it objectively, I can see that plenty of space was available had I just taken a more active role. When I look back at this time, I wish I would have realized that Libby was still there for me just as much as she was before Nick was born. She tried her best to keep me close to the family. We struggled, I struggled, but it wasn't all bad. We spent quality time together and enjoyed our weekend trips to the mountains.

Sadly, over the next few years I continued—unwittingly and unconsciously—to disconnect from Libby and myself. The most frightening aspect of this was that I didn't even realize I was drifting away. I had made great strides but then became complacent with my emotional side and neglected my emotions. Slowly the progress I had made eroded, and I once again found myself disconnected from my own feelings and emotionally distanced from Libby and Nick and from myself.

I focused on my work and grew my practice, gradually earning a solid professional reputation. From the outside looking in, I appeared to be crushing it. In reality, I was so filled with fear and anxiety at my job that I couldn't appreciate the professional success I was experiencing. The numbness was setting in professionally and personally. This state of existence was familiar to me. Even though it was horribly unhealthy, this familiarity gave me comfort. So I was lured back to the path of disconnection, burden, and resentment. I barely looked Libby in the eye anymore. I was afraid she would see that I was petrified I would fail as a provider, a father, and a husband.

> *The most frightening aspect of disconnecting was that I didn't even realize I was drifting away.*

I could not open up and expose my vulnerabilities to her, which is so essential for staying connected in an intimate relationship. Gone were the lightness and openness that we had worked hard to maintain each week in our therapy sessions. By the time Nick was in kindergarten we had gone months without any physical intimacy. Even the peck on the cheek when I came home from work was disappearing. Libby tried hard to pierce my shell of invincibility. For example, she would sit close to me when we were on the couch watching TV. I was there physically, but emotionally I wasn't.

Just like the little boy sitting next to his dad on the couch I was completely disconnected, but now I was only a danger to myself. In retrospect, I think there was a huge part of me that believed I didn't deserve to have sustained happiness with another person. I had never had that kind of relationship before. I definitely hadn't seen any examples of a loving, committed relationship growing up. In reality, most of the attention I received as a child was in the form of the abusive, secret sexual relationship with my father that filled me with shame. I was back to denying my emotions and embracing my disconnectedness. I had a good job, was married (again), and even had a child. Like before, part of me believed achieving these objective goals was all I could hope for, and my nonexistent emotional relationship with Libby was just part of life. I was drifting from my family and from myself.

> *From the outside looking in, I appeared to be crushing it. In reality, I was so filled with fear and anxiety at my job that I couldn't appreciate the professional success I was experiencing.*

Then something happened to wake me up. It was a Sunday in the spring of 2009. We had just finished watching *Harry*

Potter and the Goblet of Fire as a family, and Libby and I had put Nick to bed. I headed to our bedroom, just across the hall from Nick's room, as Libby finished up bedtime rituals with him. A few minutes later, she entered the room and confronted me with some unsavory internet history on our computer that she had discovered earlier that day. I am sure you have experienced some moment in your life when your stomach dropped out of your body. It was a combination of terror and shame at DEFCON 1. Libby was livid, crushed, and horribly confused with our relationship at that moment. At the same time, she was firmly in Mama bear mode, laser-focused on protecting Nicholas and his world.

I, too, was devastated. I had done this. I had not only broken the heart of the one person who loved me, but I had done it repeatedly. I had taken this beautiful little family I had worked so hard to build and shattered it. Shock, anger, shame, humiliation, and fear flooded in. To my thinking I had just lost everything in that instant. I felt my family was ruined and my life over.

I had no words to explain my actions to Libby. Alone in the guest room downstairs, sleep was not an option. I couldn't sit still. As I was engulfed by the physical darkness of the room and the emotional darkness of my heart and soul, the theme of failure charged back. How could I have possibly screwed this up so magnificently? I had tried to be the person I wanted to be and who Libby thought I was, thought I was doing the right thing by providing for my family, and still failed miserably. All I was focused on was my objective success of bringing home a paycheck.

Deep inside, I still believed that was all I was good for to Libby and Nicholas. I didn't think she cared about me emotionally or needed me physically. Even though I knew it was wrong succumbing to online temptations, part of me still believed I didn't matter to anyone, even myself.

The worst part was that I had allowed myself to fall right back to my comfort of isolation and selective and convenient disconnection. Instead of seeking help or sharing my feelings with Libby so we could work out our issues together, I had gone behind her back, betrayed her, neglected both her and Nicholas, and made her feel unloved. My fear and anxiety had paralyzed me emotionally. In the process, I feared I had laid waste to my life for a second time.

This second moment of profound change in my life was not as outwardly cataclysmic as the first one, but I had much more to lose this time because now I had created significant emotional bonds that I was in jeopardy of losing. I had perhaps irrevocably hurt Libby and potentially opened the door to not being in my son's life on a daily basis. I don't know what she believed or planned or thought was going to happen. I only know that after days of intense anger and avoidance, she stated that the only possible way forward would be for me to get back into therapy, to see if I could regain my emotional health and be accountable for my actions and life. If I didn't take this therapy option and try to become a better husband and father, she was going to leave with Nicholas.

Abject fear gripped me, but I lunged at the lifeline. This time, fear motivated my action instead of freezing me in place. I was not going to lose Nick. I know that sounds bad. I wish I could honestly say that losing both Libby and Nick was not an option, but that's not what I was feeling at the time. I was so lost with respect to my relationship with Libby, and I think she was even more lost, and so very angry at me, that the only motivation strong enough to pull myself out of this terrible mess was Nicholas. Fortunately, he was also the one bond between Libby and me. The one objective Libby and I shared with absolute certainty was our determination not to hurt Nicholas. We had to be better than ourselves to raise him.

Somewhere inside Libby knew that I could be a good father. She was wholly unclear about me being a good husband, but she cared so much for Nicholas that she would do anything to give him a chance to have a good family and a healthy relationship with his father. She made no promises about our relationship.

If you see some of yourself (or any period of your life) reflected in my story, I implore you to talk to someone about it. Real, meaningful change doesn't just happen, and it doesn't happen in a vacuum; it requires conscious, intentional effort and outside expertise. You don't need to understand what is wrong to engage, it's enough just to realize that you feel something is not right.

> **Pro Tip:** Find a qualified professional to work with you, to assist you in discovering and helping yourself. The professional will not solve your problems but will help you sort them out and examine your issues objectively and openly in a safe place.

> *If you see some of yourself (or any period of your life) reflected in my story, I implore you to talk to someone about it.*

Once you can take a deep breath and slow the pace of everything that is going on around you and within you, you will find that you have the answers deep inside where they always have been. Remember, if you feel off or that something is not right in your life, then something is wrong. Pay attention and set out to make it right.

FEAR DYNAMICS TECHNIQUE #7

STOP COMPARTMENTALIZING

I believe that in order to achieve professional success amid personal success, you need to eliminate this artificial divide between the two. People like to talk about their "professional life" and their "personal life" as completely separate entities. The concept of "work/life balance" has become its own industry. In actuality, professional lives and personal lives are one integral organic whole that you need to view as one contiguous life.

When I look at the world around me, it is obvious that many of us equate career success with success in life. We may even actively or unconsciously prioritize our work lives over our own personal development and over the success and happiness of our loved ones. I know I did in the past. Many marriages end and families break up because the major breadwinner is so focused on material success and supporting the family financially that he or she simply is not present enough physically, mentally, or emotionally to meet the family's demands outside the scope of finances.

Don't get me wrong. I am not judging or criticizing the breadwinners. Supporting a family in all the ways family members need and deserve to be supported is tough work, and many times the breadwinners are not getting the support they need to be successful in that role. I am only pointing out how tragic I think it is. I also believe that by following the techniques in this book, this friction can be alleviated.

> *In actuality, professional lives and personal lives are one integral organic whole that you need to view as one contiguous life.*

While we are frantically trying to keep pace on the ever-accelerating treadmill of life, we often assume, falsely, that we do not have the time, energy, or money to invest in personal development or individual therapy or couples therapy or family therapy. We think, again falsely, that the time we invest in those areas of our lives subtracts from the time and energy we have to invest in our careers. Investment for the betterment of our core self often has the best return on investment of all. We try to achieve "a balanced life" by flipping channels—compartmentalizing. We focus on work at work and focus on family at home, and that may work for a while to a certain degree, but at some point the system will break down.

Make Home and Work a Continuum

I think a much more effective way to achieve a healthier coexistence with the many worlds you interact with is to blur the line between home and work, between personal and professional. Simply put, it is one life, there is no balancing. As I began to understand and integrate the issues in my past and how the fear and anxiety from them played out in my personal life, I noticed a dramatic improvement in my personal life. I was able to put into action all the Fear Dynamics Techniques. However, while things were on the uptick outside of work, I continued to struggle with fear and anxiety in the workplace. While it seems obvious now, I didn't realize at the time that all the skills I had acquired by working on my personal development could also benefit me in my career. I just needed to transfer those skills to my work. I had to stop compartmentalizing.

> *Investment for the betterment of our core self often has the best return on investment of all.*

My job is stressful, as most jobs are, especially if you are committed to excellence, but in some ways that commitment can diminish performance. I felt as though I always needed to have the answer to every question and the solution to every problem right at my fingertips. I believed that if I failed to meet this self-imposed (and unrealistic) standard, I would be a failure, a fraud, and would be fired. If this sounds familiar, you may be suffering anxiety in the workplace too. When I began my career as a lawyer, I would never have told a client, "I'm not sure what we should do next" or "Let me track down an expert on this so we can be sure to consider all possible plans of action" or simply "I don't know." I did what many service professionals and management people do—I masked uncertainty with overconfidence.

> *I didn't realize that all the skills I had acquired by working on my personal development could also benefit me in my career. I just needed to transfer those skills to my work. I had to stop compartmentalizing.*

My anxiety levels increased exponentially as my job responsibilities expanded and increased in complexity. I was performing well professionally and hitting all objective markers of success, but internally I was a mess and lived in a constant state of tension, believing it all was about to collapse at any given moment. I was stressed out all the time at work and didn't even realize the extent of my anxiety until I began to really dig into my professional issues in psychotherapy.

As I was starting to reflect internally with some degree of objectivity, I realized that many of the issues with my fear, anxiety, and self-esteem in my personal life were also clearly present in my daily working life. I finally made the connection that the work environment is really just another set of relationships—certainly different from relationships with family members and friends, but all human. I soon learned the fallacy of a separate work life and family life. As I was working on being accountable in my personal life and changing the way I interacted with and experienced that world, I realized that I also could change the way I engaged in my law practice and be much more satisfied in the workplace. It sounds so simple, yet for me this realization was revolutionary.

I had assembled a set of simple processes to manage my anxiety and fear on a social/personal level, so I began to apply these techniques to my work. First, I had to accept myself as I was, not as the all-knowing, all-powerful being I falsely assumed people expected me to be (Fear Dynamics Technique #1, page 14). Second, I built in a pause to give myself time to think and respond with greater deliberation (Fear Dynamics Technique #4, page 48). Third, I created and used decision trees to ensure answers and solutions were based on facts and logic (Fear Dynamics Technique #5, page 71).

Don't Expect a Smooth Transition

Initially, the Fear Dynamics Techniques I had developed did not transfer automatically from my personal to my professional life, and my transformation at work did not occur overnight. I had to put in the same kind of effort in my professional life as I had done in my personal life to make a difference. At first I would have to pause after a call with a client and completely replay the discussion to analyze it in hindsight. I had to identify my emotions and examine them closely to determine whether my anxiety during the call was rational or irrational in the context of what we discussed. I would then work through the decision tree to determine whether the advice I offered was fact-based and logical.

This process forced me to examine my interactions with other professionals and evaluate my thoughts and behaviors objectively to understand what was causing me to think, act, and express myself as I did. I discovered that in many interactions I had acted irrationally. As you can imagine, this led to more self-examination, mirror-gazing, and psychotherapy.

Once I engaged in this baseline exercise for a bit, building in a pause and consulting my decision tree quickly became second nature. I no longer needed to pause to self-evaluate, now I could do it on the fly and in real time. I began to trust my emotions in the moment and engaged more energetically, spontaneously, and confidently in all areas of my practice and profession.

> *I had to put in the same kind of effort in my professional life as I had done in my personal life to make a difference.*

In fact, I realized that I enjoyed being a lawyer, dealing with (most) clients, and handling challenging projects. I was blessed to work with interesting people and projects daily and had constant opportunities to learn. I had a renewed passion for my profession and an appreciation of my ability to engage at a high level without it taking an unreasonable toll on me physically, emotionally, and mentally. I can talk all day long about how much better I felt and the difference I perceived in my practice, but I also have empirical evidence.

I had a good practice before 2009, but as I look back on the last fifteen years or so, my practice has steadily grown in terms of the complexity of projects, number of clients, financial success, and professional reputation. I now engage in highly complex matters routinely and am often sought out as a subject-matter expert and as a speaker at industry events. This was not the case before I examined myself and actively changed how I acted and interacted professionally.

Today, I do not dread the phone calls or emails I get (other than when I have good reason to dread the communication).

I have no problem responding to questions without feeling as though I am being attacked or expected to know the answer on any topic even if it is well outside my wheelhouse or experience. I feel comfortable in my uncertainty and can easily tell a client, "I'm not sure what we should do here, give me a few days to think about it." That is not to say that my job is free of fear and anxiety. What's new is that I now understand and recognize fear dynamics. I can tell the difference between rational and irrational fear and anxiety and identify the source of those feelings. It is not undifferentiated anxiety.

> *I now engage in highly complex matters routinely and am often sought out as a subject-matter expert and as a speaker at industry events. This was not the case before I examined myself and actively changed how I acted and interacted professionally.*

I understand why I am anxious because of a deadline looming, a new fact that throws a deal into question, or some other normal, random free-range particle that often arises in the world of business. Being able to know what is causing the stress and anxiety may not alleviate the anxiety, but it does enable me to be calm and focused as I address the issue and not wander aimlessly, overwhelmed, unable to determine what needs to be done, and wondering why I am anxious.

Set Realistic Expectations for Yourself

I have also learned through my reflection and analysis of my work world that I am not responsible for everything that happens on a deal or with a client. I cannot divine everything or immediately correct an unexpected wrong turn. I now try to view my client relationships more like "The Property Brothers" on HGTV. It seems that in every episode, once the remodeling project gets underway, they discover some unknown problem that makes the remodel more complicated and more expensive. Nobody ever says to the brothers, "Hey man, how come you didn't know about the faulty wiring in the attic?" The homeowners always give Drew and Jonathan a chance to solve the issue and modify the plans. The homeowners may not be happy with the circumstance, but they are not angry with the brothers and do not blame them for the issue.

> *For the most part, people are reasonable, and if you can set aside your own irrational fears and anxiety that you need to have all the answers immediately, you likely will find yourself much happier in your work life.*

I have come to realize that clients and colleagues don't expect me to anticipate and solve all issues before they happen or immediately upon their discovery, and if they do, they are being unreasonable. Most clients understand that some time may be needed to unpack a complicated issue that arose due to an unforeseen fact or circumstance. Regardless of your job or profession, I think that most people engage in this manner. Even the most intense and demanding business environments allow for reflection and value thoughtful approaches to problems.

There may be time crunches, but the people involved, if they actually pause for a moment, will want to get a meaningful response rather than just a quick one to placate them for a second. For the most part, people are reasonable, and if you can set aside your own irrational fears and anxiety that you need to have all the answers immediately, you likely will find yourself much happier in your work life.

Once I became more comfortable with myself in the workplace, I also became attuned to the fear dynamics of my professional life, and it allowed me to work more fluidly and productively. For example, I was working with an outside accountant and during a conference call an unexpected question came up. In response, he tried to brush off the issue with supreme confidence and then aggressively pushed for a decision to be made based on prior facts and known risks, although there were several outstanding new issues that could affect the analysis. I gently pushed back on his conclusory statements and advised the client to pause before moving forward to get some clarity on all the issues.

That allowed all of us to take a deep breath and slow down. The next time we spoke (three hours later), the accountant's demeanor differed dramatically, and he answered questions with depth and nuance. He had taken the speed bump opportunity and dug into the issues to fully understand the new facts and how they changed his analysis.

> *My inner work has shown me that you cannot separate your personal life from your work life. It is all life.*

In the first conversation his anxiety impaired his ability to provide advice and assurance. Once he was able to regroup and analyze the issue, he was able to respond confidently. A few months later I learned that he was promoted from junior partner to full partner in his firm and that the deal we worked on together had been his first engagement as lead on a transaction.

My inner work has shown me that you cannot separate your personal life from your work life. It is all life. It has also shown me that in business, we are all still human, even if sometimes people pretend not to be. Our humanness is inescapable. Just like our personal lives, our work lives are all about relationships and connections.

Pro Tip: My advice is to embrace your own humanity, as well as the humanity of those you encounter in the professional world, whether they're colleagues, clients, or adversaries. I firmly believe that this attitude will make your work more fulfilling and make you happier and more successful.

Chapter 7

SAVING MY FAMILY, SAVING MYSELF

t was almost light out the next morning when I dragged myself out of bed and slinked out of the house to go to work. I slept little that night, during which I had experienced a fleeting moment of thinking the whole episode was a dream. But that was before the daunting reality flooded over me. My life today was different from my life yesterday. I had spent the majority of the night catastrophizing the details of my life in shambles: No son, no wife, living in a cheap apartment, and struggling to see my son whenever I could. Being "that guy." Every cliché about a mid-life divorced man played in IMAX clarity over and over in the private theatre of my brain. Had I ruined my son with my actions? Could I possibly regain my wife's trust? Had I once again sabotaged my life? What's wrong with me?

I could have thrown myself into my work and decided to focus on saving that part of my life since, at the time, it seemed unlikely

I would be able to salvage any meaningful pieces of my personal life. But there was a part of me that embraced this fear of losing my family because it motivated me. For the first time, fear moved me to take action instead of paralyzing me. My fear and anxiety had gotten me into this spot and, ironically, it was the initial driver to get me out of it. I knew I cared deeply about my family and somehow I cared enough about part of me that I wanted to work to keep my family together.

I decided not to avoid this morass of emotional pain and instead became grateful for it because it showed me that I was not completely disconnected from my family or myself. I decided I was going to wade back into the waters of therapy and dedicate myself to the process. But first, I needed to find the right therapist.

I had worked with therapists before and they were helpful in their own way, but I had never been this motivated. People always say, "This time is different." Well, for me, this time was different. The stakes were real. It was not just me that was at risk. Now it was my son. He deserved to have a good father and a stable and supportive family. I chose to have him, and I was failing him as a father. I knew, even at this chaotic point, that if I focused on Nick I would be able to dig deeper than I had in the past and work harder on myself. I had to do what I could to make his life the best it could be.

I called the couples therapist Libby and I worked with a few years prior and asked her if she had any referrals for me to see. I let her know that I had regressed emotionally and that the issues we touched on in our couples therapy were deeply affecting me, and that I had severely hurt Libby and our family. She gave me two recommendations. My heart leapt. There was a chance.

I called both referrals and was shocked by how different my reactions were to them. Even though I was emotionally discombobulated, I still had an effective internal radar for evaluating people. The first therapist I spoke to was a man who spoke with an air of authority from the beginning of the phone call. I briefly described my situation, including my history and current crisis. From the first sentence out of his mouth, I was on edge. I felt that this person was already judging me. I was immediately filled with even more shame than before I had called him.

> *For the first time, fear moved me to take action instead of paralyzing me.*

He seemed to ramble on about how much pain I caused people and that there was no way to tell if I could fix things. All of this was true, of course, but in that moment I was doing enough self-flagellating that I did not need someone else to pile it on. I wasn't looking for forgiveness from him, but immediate and ill-informed judgment was also not what I needed. He explained his office hours and where he was located. As he droned on with administrative matters, I barely heard him as my heart sank.

I was not sure what I had expected but realized that I could not work with this person. My catastrophic thinking kicked in as I felt that all hope was lost. I was never going to be with my son again, all of the destruction I played in my mind over the past few days was actually going to happen. I mumbled that I would look at my schedule and see what may work for a visit and quickly ended the call. As I hung up the phone, all I felt was despair.

A few hours later, the second therapist called me back. She explained that she had been working with patients and other matters during the day and this was her time to return calls. I repeated my summary as I had with the other candidate and then paused. Waiting. I had conditioned myself that she would judge me harshly, shame me, and drive home how I had most likely ruined my life and the lives of my family. Instead, she said, "I can only imagine the pain and confusion you must be feeling." Simple, straight to the point, and no qualitative commentary. I did not know what to say. I simply said, "Yes, it is overwhelming. I feel lost."

She went on to say that she believed that she may be able to help me, but she would need to learn more and that we should schedule a session to meet in person. A moment of calm. Someone who heard a small part of how horrible I was and did not discard me, did not hammer home the shame. This person took in the facts and was going to see if she could help me. I took the next available appointment: 2 pm the following afternoon. I did not even look at my calendar, I would clear my schedule of any conflicts.

> **Pro Tip:** I tell you this story so you persevere in finding the right therapist for you. He or she is out there—someone that you resonate with and who can guide you on your emotional health path.

The next day was a glorious Colorado spring day— the kind of day that makes people say, "This is why I love Colorado." The sun was out, not a cloud in the blue-bird sky, mid-70s and no humidity. Everything was greening up, birds were chirping, and the air was alive and vibrant. But for me, I plodded through the day as if I were wrapped in Siberian cold and fog. I was trepidatious about this meeting with the therapist. I know it was foolish but I was hoping that, now that I had hit rock bottom, a simple fix could be found. I would soon learn this was the furthest thing from the truth. But, for now, I at least had some hope of a path forward.

This therapist worked from her home. I arrived far too early, so I parked and walked around the neighborhood a bit. It was an older area with mature trees but still in a bustling part of Denver. The sidewalks meandered passed homes from different eras, some original, others newer builds. I struggled to reconcile the calm surroundings and beautiful day with the shame and fear I felt.

> *I know it was foolish but I was hoping that, now that I had hit rock bottom, a simple fix could be found. I would soon learn this was the furthest thing from the truth. But, for now, I at least had some hope of a path forward.*

As my appointment time neared, I made my way back to her home office. A flagstone path guided me through an overgrown garden to a back entrance to her home. I felt a little as though I was entering a war bunker as I walked down the set of red brick stairs, but that was probably due to my state of mind. The waiting room was cozy. Too anxious to sit I perused the books on the shelves. It was an eclectic mix of professional books and fiction. Little did I realize at the time, but I would end up reading several of these books in two- to three-page increments over the coming years as I waited for appointments.

The therapist came out of a door on the side wall and ushered me into her office. I was so overcome with shame that I did not look up. I could not make eye contact. Even with the little I had told her I assumed she was judging me, and I could almost not bear to be in the room with her. In those first moments I was so filled with fear and anxiety the only thoughts I had were that this will never work. I felt that I should leave immediately and tell Libby I am broken and will never be what she and Nick deserve. I thought, *Why waste this person's time? I am irredeemable, shattered beyond repair.*

But when she asked me to sit down so we could talk, I complied. I looked everywhere but at her. Her office was exactly what you would expect a therapist's office to be. Bookshelves covered an entire wall and a half. Two chairs facing each other and, stereotypically, a couch clearly designed for patients to lay down on, Freudian style. Inside I thought, *I am never going to lay on that couch.* I was wrong. Over the next few years, I became very familiar with the intricacies of the ceiling tile in that office. There also was a good-sized table serving as a desk, and along one wall, a fireplace. I never saw an actual fire in it, but the fireplace finished the room perfectly.

The room was in the basement of the house so there was one window high on the exterior wall that looked out onto ground level. During my time with her, I have seen cats, squirrels, rabbits, and other patients' feet through that window. What I recall most vividly when I think about that little window is the passing of seasons.

I quickly got into a pattern of going early in the morning. In the fall and winter I started my session in the dark and watched the light of day creep through the window with swirling leaves or snow. In the spring and summer my sessions began with early daylight shining through the window with the promise of a warm day ahead. It is not lost on me the irony of how pleasant that window in Denver was for me over the years in contrast to the similar basement window in my house in Plover, Wisconsin, where I could not recall seeing anything through that window the entire time I lived there.

> *Over the next few years, I became very familiar with the intricacies of the ceiling tile in that office.*

The first day we spoke I gave her a full recitation of my history. I was determined not to leave out any detail that I thought was harmful or that drove my shame. Rather than trying to sugarcoat my history, I went in the opposite direction and tried to tell her everything. I was hell-bent on making sure she knew how bad a person I was. I felt as though I was trying to prove to her why the events happening to me were justified and that I deserved what was happening to me. I also believe that at some core level I wanted to make sure that she knew I was committed to the process and not going to omit any facts.

When I paused for a breath after my recitation of horribles, she simply stated that she felt she could help me and that she believed me when I said I wanted to work on what was tearing me up inside. She did not diagnose me or give me a timeline. She gave me her credentials and said that given my agitated state, she recommended that we meet often for the foreseeable future. I was not prepared for that suggestion. I was trained by popular culture that you saw a shrink once a week and that was how it worked. Now, she was telling me that I needed to talk with her as many days a week as possible, but a minimum of four to start.

> *When I paused for a breath after my recitation of horribles, she simply stated that she felt she could help me and that she believed me when I said I wanted to work on what was tearing me up inside.*

Although I was stunned, her suggestion validated me and my situation and I readily agreed. Just in the hour I spoke with her I found relief in letting loose my flurry of thoughts and feelings. I was desperate, highly motivated, and hoped the more weekly sessions I had, the sooner I would get "better."

In that basement I began my journey to emotional well-being. I know it sounds corny or trite, but starting there I forged new pathways to becoming a happy, healthy person. I've spent thousands of hours over the last several years creating new ways to react to situations and plans to combat stress and anxiety. I needed to tell myself it was okay to want to be happy and to work to be happy. If I was going to grind on the other aspects of "success," I needed to prioritize my personal happiness in the same way.

FEAR DYNAMICS TECHNIQUE #8

DON'T BE A DUCK

When I restarted therapy in earnest in 2009, it felt different to me than the previous times I had attempted personal growth. For the first time I had something I was fighting for that was beyond myself. Then I had the realization of self-acceptance that I discussed in Fear Dynamics Technique #1 (page 14). When I internalized the fact that I was made up of all parts of my past and that the point where I was at this moment in time was acceptable, it lightened the load of therapy. I was able to see incremental progress and keep my focus on daily growth instead of this nebulous end point of being a fully-developed mentally and emotionally healthy guy.

During therapy I spent significant time thinking and talking about my childhood. One image I vividly remember from my childhood is ducks serenely cruising the Wisconsin River behind my house nearly every day. Or so it appeared to me. It never occurred to me that just below the water's surface they were paddling like mad to get where they wanted to be, despite the ever-flowing current pushing them downstream. I was unable to see just how much effort they were exerting. Later, a colleague of mine called my attention to a condition often referred to as *duck syndrome*, in which people appear to be calm on the surface but are frantically trying to keep pace with the demands on their lives.

Often people use this metaphor to describe teens in high pressure academic situations during which they pretend to be in control of their lives when, in reality, they are working feverishly in secret. My wife attended an elite university where kids would brag that they didn't even need to crack a book before their Accelerated Multivariable Calculus final exam when, in reality, they had studied nonstop for the greater part of the seventy-two hours leading up to the exam. Teens are not the only ones who suffer from this syndrome; in fact, they learn it from adults. When I looked back over my life, I realized I was a duck, and I had been a duck my entire life and did not even know it.

Don't Hide Behind a Public Persona

One of my primary lifelong struggles was working to create a public persona of controlled perfection. My parents ingrained in me that, above all else, the world must perceive us as normal, content, and completely in control of our lives. So, in addition to having to deal with a nightmare existence of neglect and abuse from my parents, I was trained to pretend that I came from the happiest of families.

My entire life was a facade. As you might imagine, this instilled a continuous cycle of increasing stress, fear, and anxiety in me. I cannot remember how many times my mom would call me into their bedroom before I left for school to manage her hangover. Recovering from last night's Manhattans, slurring her words, she would tell me to call her assistant, Sandy, and say she was sick and could not teach that day. I suppose she *was* sick; she certainly was in no condition to lecture to her child psychology class about the importance of nurturing infants with affection.

You would think these calls would have become easier to make, but each time I was nervous dialing the number and having to lie to Sandy about my mom's non-descript illness. I am pretty sure Sandy knew I was lying, but we both played our parts and exchanged the usual pleasantries, and Sandy wished my mother a speedy recovery. I dreaded making those calls, but keeping up the facade of functionality was most important.

> *My entire life was a facade. As you might imagine, this instilled a continuous cycle of increasing stress, fear, and anxiety in me.*

My parents wanted people to think they were involved with their kids but they rarely attended sporting events or school programs. When they did, they never seemed to go together. One of my parents would dutifully drive me to the event and then sit away from the crowd and impatiently wait for the ordeal to end. My parents did not interact with the other families and we would quietly return to the car after the event and head home in silence. I recall, though, how when my parents were forced to talk to others about attending these events they did so not with joy in their voices, but more with a tone conveying the drudgery of fulfilling traditional parental duties.

Holidays were bad. I already mentioned the Bataan Death March of cookie-making when we all would trudge through creating holiday treats—sans merriment—so that my dad could take a beautiful tray to the office to show off his family's Christmas tradition. A while ago I saw a photo of our traditional Christmas Eve dinner of Cornish hens with orange sauce. In the photo my mom is wearing her holiday bathrobe and is already zoned out from alcohol, and we children are staring at the camera absent any holiday glee. But my dad took that photo every year to record our beautiful holiday dinner to reinforce the facade of our family's happiness. As if taking a picture that was supposed to represent family happiness would conjure that reality or, at a minimum, stand as evidence of it to the rest of the world.

The special outings with my dad were even worse. My friends were so impressed when, in 1983, my dad took me to see the Green Bay Packers play on a Monday night. I smiled and agreed what a thoughtful dad I had, while feeling disgusted inside remembering how he molested me in the hotel room after the game.

As I suspect is true in many families, we were all very committed to projecting the appearance of normalcy to the outside world. I grew up full of fear and anxiety that people would find out that we as a family were not perfect. My mother was an authority on child psychology and my dad went on to become the chair of the Theology Department at Boston College. They presented the charade of the Cleaver, Cunningham, or Huxtable family (depending on your TV era), but we all knew the truth. This split with reality was monumentally confusing to me.

Sometimes I didn't even know what was real and what was a lie. I was ashamed of my family and embarrassed by the lies I told, but my parents never acknowledged that their actions were at all "inappropriate," nor did anyone outside our nuclear family appear to notice. Nobody was there to help me recognize all this dysfunction.

I felt horrible at home, afraid of being alone with my father and disregarded by my mother. I had a secret to keep at all costs. Everyone in my family hid unpleasant truths. It was normal to have dual lives and disguise family dysfunction behind a veneer of normalcy. I couldn't see that my family was unhealthy. I assumed all families were like mine.

Inside I was emotionally detached and disconnected. The emotional pain was too great to fully experience. I could not understand my feelings or talk about them. I needed to escape the emotions somehow so that I could at least function. My path was to disconnect, not feel my emotions, and create a separate person for the world to see and for me to be. I did not reach the point of experiencing dissociative identity disorder (having two or more distinct identities with different names), but it came close to that, and I can see how that could happen. I don't know why I didn't drink or do drugs to numb my feelings. Maybe part of me just didn't want to be anything like my parents. It wasn't as though I was making conscious choices about who I wanted to be or what I wanted to do. It was instinctive.

> I couldn't see that my family was unhealthy. I assumed all families were like mine.

For me, this profound disconnect resulted in a chasm between my personal reality and my public persona. I could not be myself either at home or outside my home. My true self was denied at home, and I had to deny my self in public to maintain appearances of normalcy. My parents did not instill in me a belief that I was special and interesting, so I felt worthless, and because I felt worthless, I felt the need to create a separate, fictional persona—one I thought the world would think was special and interesting and worth noticing.

When I was a little guy, I would fake injuries at school. Before leaving home, I would meticulously wrap up my arm in an ace bandage and play up my injury to my teacher and classmates to get attention. Then I would show how special I was by still being able to play "King of the Hill" on a snow pile in winter. I thought it showed how powerful I was, but what it really proved was that my injury was fake. Nobody ever called me out on this but looking back, I bet my teachers and classmates laughed behind my back.

In college, I continued to tell lies in an attempt to elevate how special and important I was because I thought it was the only way anyone would want to be with me. I used to tell people I worked as a clerk in a law office when I really worked at Arby's. To make myself appear more interesting I told people that I saw Keanu Reeves at the airport. It still embarrasses me that the first time I met my wife, I told her I had a tryout to be a kicker for the San Francisco 49ers. In retrospect, it is apparent that she knew this was an obvious lie, but she still saw something in me that was lovable.

In telling these lies I was trying to convince people that I was special and that they should want to be with me and see I had worth. I was starved for someone to want me, and I felt I needed to be someone different from who I was. Sadly, just being me was not enough.

Recognizing the Personal Costs of Faking It

Many of us inadvertently create puffed up versions of ourselves. You might tell someone you're trying to impress that you are looking at the new Mercedes S 560, when you are really going to buy a used Honda CRX, or that you just returned from the latest Rosewood resort in Mexico when you really had a staycation, or that your daughter is excelling in high school, when in fact, she is barely making it, or that you really love your job when each day you count the minutes until you can leave the office.

Our son has played competitive tennis since he was young, which has brought us into contact with many outwardly "chill" parents who are actually strung tighter than their kid's tennis racquet. You know these _____ parents (*insert your sport of choice*). They will nonchalantly say, "Oh, junior just plays for the fun of the game and to get some exercise," when everyone knows they're dropping thousands of dollars on private lessons and high-level drill academies. Or they're logging every unforced error their kid makes on some NASA-level software for tennis. When their kid doesn't perform as expected or hoped you can see the steam escape from their ears as they politely excuse themselves to excoriate their ten-year-old in the privacy of their car.

You do not need to maintain these pretenses.

Throughout most of my life, I was filled with fear and anxiety that no one would love the real me. I had slipped back into that place during my second marriage even though I knew deep down that my wife and son did know and love the real me—at least the part of me that I let them see. Many of us who grew up in less-than-ideal homes struggle with these issues, and we all develop different coping mechanisms. While many of these coping techniques—such as creating an inauthentic public persona—are socially acceptable, they often come at great personal cost. This false image is a lie to hide the shame, but it subtly reinforces the shame instead of alleviating it. To avoid the shame, we continue the cycle by lying more and disconnecting even more from reality.

> *While many of these coping techniques—such as creating an inauthentic public persona—are socially acceptable, they often come at great personal cost.*

Be Real

I am not advocating that you lay yourself bare and share your deepest secrets and most crushing humiliations with strangers. What I am suggesting with this Fear Dynamics Technique is that you try to be real with yourself and authentic in your interactions with others. How? Whenever I notice myself feeling the urge to misrepresent my reality, I pause long enough to take a breath, during which time I check in with myself to make sure that the way I am about to respond is genuine.

Have you ever told a lie about something that was inconsequential? Maybe you told the lie to someone you were sitting next to on a plane and would never see again. Or maybe you embellished a story to make yourself look better to someone who really could not have cared less. Later, you probably wondered why you had told the lie or embellished the story. What I am suggesting is that instead of wondering about it later—and perhaps feeling guilty about it—you pause to consider, just for a split second before opening your mouth, and decide to speak only truth. As you practice this, the conscious effort will fade away and you will fluidly become genuine.

> *What we have in common is the fact that we all struggle, and we should celebrate that common thread that ties us all together as human beings.*

With this technique, the next tool I use to help myself be real is reminding myself that **we are all in this together**. This is a fundamental shift I made in my world view and it has made a tremendous difference. My parents raised me to believe that no one, not even myself, should know my pain. They also taught me that connections with other people would only lead to disappointment. I grew up believing that other people were happy and successful and interesting and that I could be an engaging participant only if I hid my real self. I realized I needed to shift this paradigm of fear.

Pro Tip: One pivotal realization I made is that everyone out there is struggling. It is part of being human, part of our everyday existence, and essential for growth.

My struggle may be wildly different from yours, and that's okay. What we have in common is the fact that we all struggle, and we should celebrate that common thread that ties us all together as human beings. Instead, we pretend that we are crushing it in every aspect of our lives. What we should do is admit to ourselves, and others, that sometimes we stumble. We grow, we learn, and then we pick ourselves up and try again.

> *I help myself be real by reminding myself that we are all in this together.*

This realization helps make us more forgiving of ourselves and others. It also closes the space that divides us so we can work more closely to achieve happiness and self-fulfillment. Life is so much easier, richer, and fuller when we work together. We are all in this together, we all struggle, and we all need help.

Now when I see a duck, I smile because I know that I am in control of both my public persona and my own personal reality. Sometimes I know I have to paddle hard to resist and navigate the currents, but sometimes I can just relax, float, and enjoy the scenery.

Chapter 8

FEAR DYNAMICS AT WORK AND AT HOME

O ver the course of my self-improvement program, I began to notice a transformation happening, not only within myself and in my personal relationships, but also in my professional relationships and my ability to counsel clients and guide them through complex transactions. Much of my work involves negotiating business mergers and acquisitions, which entail exchanging valuable assets and often relinquishing control over a business that an individual, group, or family has built from the ground up.

Emotions can heat up, triggering one or more participants to revert to counterproductive patterns of thought and behavior. Fear of loss and of the unknown can often stir anxiety and distrust, negatively impacting individuals and their interactions. In addition to our personal lives I have given significant thought to the way fear impacts our professional lives. People do not acknowledge the importance of fear dynamics in the workplace. It can erode working relationships until they cannot be salvaged.

Fear is an unpleasant feeling that tells us when someone or something is potentially dangerous—that it threatens our safety or well-being or is likely to cause pain of some sort. It serves the useful purpose of keeping us out of trouble. It can motivate us to take much-needed action—fight, flight, or freeze. And it is useful in various aspects of our lives, warning us of threats not only in the physical world, but also in our personal or business relationships, our careers, our finances, or even our freedom.

However, if it is unwarranted or excessive, fear can warp perception, stifle innovation, erode confidence, undermine trust, and trigger conflict. Left unchecked or misunderstood it can paralyze an individual or an entire organization and lead people to make poor decisions with potentially catastrophic consequences. Yet, fear in the business environment is rarely addressed in any formal way. In fact, most people in the business world do not even recognize the warning signs. As a result, many individuals and organizations suffer the consequences—chronic stress, diminished productivity, lost opportunities/promotions, and stagnation to name a few.

The good news is that individuals and organizations crippled by fear can begin to optimize their performance by becoming more mindful of fear in the workplace and by developing techniques to challenge their fears and disrupt the destructive cycle of fear-based behaviors and interactions.

Fear can warp perception, stifle innovation, erode confidence, undermine trust, and trigger conflict.

Fear on Two Levels

Fear operates on two levels—individual and group (two or more people). When fear strikes an individual, it can make the individual combative, detached, or paralyzed. For example, in a professional setting if your current workload makes you feel overwhelmed, you may be too afraid to think critically, push for the correct solution, and pursue an easier path. You have so much to do you cannot figure out where to start, so you freeze up. If someone asks you to do something or hands you another assignment you may blow up and say something sarcastic to blow off steam, such as "Sure, why not?!"

> *The key is understanding that one or more actors are being affected by fear and that is playing out in the group relational dynamic.*

On the personal side, say in a new intimate relationship, fear of rejection can make you pick a fight, blow off a date, or be unable to move the relationship forward.

On the group level, when one or more people are afraid, their fear bleeds over into the rest of the group, negatively impacting interactions between individuals. I started to refer to this as fear dynamics, specifically, the behavior and communication patterns that emerge during interpersonal interactions involving the fear or the anxiety of all involved parties.

The genesis of the fear and the related anxiety is not important at this level of interaction. The key is understanding that one or more actors are being affected by fear and that is playing out in the group relational dynamic. Fear dynamics can be insidious in a corporate setting as well as in a family.

For example, I was working with a client who wanted to team up with another party to purchase and become partners in a business. One party had the skill and operational knowledge, while the other party had the opportunity and capital. Acting together they had the potential to create something unique and greater than the sum of their two parts, something greater than either of them could accomplish individually.

> *Fear dynamics can be insidious in a corporate setting as well as in a family.*

Unfortunately, the initial excitement and energy was quickly infected by anxiety and fear. The party with the opportunity and capital recognized the value and necessity of the other party's skill and operational knowledge and began to feel threatened by it—that he would somehow be ousted from the partnership or be relegated to serving as a silent partner and would lose his right to participate. Instead of discussing his anxiety openly, he refused to go along with certain terms of the agreement out of fear that he would expose himself to this risk.

The other party (with the skill and operational knowledge) interpreted this hesitancy as a power play instead of as anxiety. Instead of working to understand the underlying cause of his prospective partner's reluctance to agree to certain terms, she shut down and started to use phrases like "take it or leave it," which only reinforced the other party's existing fears of being shut out.

Unfortunately, in such situations, potential deals often fall apart, but neither party is usually directly to blame. The blame should be placed on the fear dynamics and the failure of the two parties to recognize and address it. Neither party can take a step back and look at the situation with some objectivity and reflection. When deals fall apart due to fear dynamics I find the situation tragic.

Certainly, there are times when two people should just not do a deal; some people cannot and probably should not work together. However, I have seen more cases in which people who are a great fit emotionally and culturally, and who have a great idea for a joint project, struggle or fail to execute it because fear dynamics begin to swirl and are not mitigated or managed. As a result, the fear dynamics escalate in intensity to the point of being unmanageable and the project dies.

In personal relationships, fear dynamics may be easier to identify because we expect these relationships to have an emotional component, but that doesn't mean they are any easier to unravel. They may even be knottier because your personal vulnerability is on the line. When my wife and I were struggling years ago, we were deeply mired in fear dynamics. I was so disconnected from myself and from her that she responded by building up her own personal wall of protection.

Before your relationship reaches that point, I suggest you use Fear Dynamics Technique #3 of making eye contact (page 40). When you make and hold eye contact with a loved one, it forces you to be in the moment as well as vulnerable with each other. Allowing this vulnerability helps to dissipate the fear between you and your loved one and then allows you to engage in genuine and rational thought. Eye contact can be equally effective in a business discussion to create trust and genuineness in the interaction.

Managing Fear Dynamics

The fear in fear dynamics is the same feeling evoked in any frightening situation you may face alone, but dynamics come into play only when other people are affected by the fear. In other words, fear dynamics has a relational aspect to it. For example, in the workplace, if you're afraid to share ideas with colleagues outside of work because a supervisor perceives such interactions as a threat, your supervisor's fear is creating a negative dynamic between the two of you, inhibiting your ability to innovate and communicate with colleagues and, as a result, is harming the organization overall. In a personal relationship, fear dynamics cause relationships to stagnate, then wither, and ultimately die.

When fear operates unchecked or unacknowledged in an organization or in a relationship, people often respond in the following ways. Be on the lookout for these behaviors at work and at home. When people are caught up in the dynamics of fear, they may:

- Stop asking questions
- Show little to no interest in innovating or sharing ideas or information
- Disengage with colleagues, clients, friends, and family members
- Ignore or downplay problems and mistakes
- Discourage or disregard new ideas or suggestions
- Make more mistakes or forget agreed-upon responsibilities

- Blame others
- Instigate or engage in conflict
- Undermine initiatives or new directions in a relationship
- Leave

As a result, individuals, organizations, and personal relationships suffer. In the professional realm, here is a short list of the many ways individuals and organizations suffer from the effects of unacknowledged and poorly managed fear:

- Stagnation sets in, slowing or shutting down adaptation to ever-changing market conditions
- Productivity drops as people lose motivation and engage in unproductive and counterproductive activities
- Collaboration gives way to internal competition and conflict as trust erodes
- Potentially lucrative deals and partnerships are undermined
- Absenteeism increases in direct correlation with stress levels
- Malaise and disregard for others in an organization or a group increase, resulting in dehumanization
- Turnover increases as frustrated employees look for the exits
- Organizations become more reactive than proactive, leading to poor decision-making
- An organization's risk tolerance declines, negatively impacting innovation

Perhaps what is most sinister about fear dynamics in the workplace is that they most often arise from unseen causes. Like a tsunami that swells from shifting land masses miles below sea level, fear dynamics wash over everyone involved, often without them ever sensing the cause. Fortunately, you can mitigate the damage and restore a healthy dynamic in your relationships before the fear dynamic causes too much damage—assuming you are able to engage calmly, even if you do not know what is really going on beneath the surface.

In a personal relationship, fear dynamics has eroded your relationship when both parties feel unheard, disregarded, and alone. In my relationship with my wife the disconnection may have originated with me because of my fear that she didn't have room in her heart for both me and our young son and my overarching work anxiety. But my wife responded to my lack of emotional participation in the relationship by building up her own walls to protect herself from feelings of rejection caused by my behaviors.

My hope is that reading this book will help you identify the early stages of fear dynamics in the work place and in your personal relationships. Here are four steps for analyzing and addressing fear dynamics.

Step 1: *Recognize the Symptoms of Fear Dynamics*

The first step to managing fear dynamics is to identify any thoughts and behaviors that may be motivated by fear. Any irrational thought or behavior is suspect. For example, if someone is being more combative than is usual for that person, or more combative than is necessary in a given situation, begin to question that person's motivation. Here are a few of the most common warning signs that fear is influencing a person's behavior or a group dynamic (some of these are specific to a business environment):

- **Peculiar behavior or communication:** Someone is acting peculiar or out of character or is communicating in ways that undermine the collective effort to achieve a positive outcome.
- **Lack of communication:** People appear reluctant to say what they think, or nobody's talking.
- **Self-deprecation:** Someone is belittling their own value, which is a classic sign of insecurity, typically caused by an underlying fear, such as fear of rejection.
- **Lack of eye contact:** This could be a sign that someone is hiding something or is afraid to express an idea or a desire.
- **Lack of motivation and innovation:** People are naturally creative and generous unless they are afraid.
- **Excessive carbon copying of email messages:** When personnel carbon copy (cc) superiors excessively they are usually insecure either with their own ideas or in how ideas are received and developed.
- **Explosive outbursts, especially from leadership:** Fear is often expressed as anger, which evokes more fear. When leadership is the source of the outbursts you can be certain that the organization, or at least the group, is operating in a culture of fear.
- **Inability to admit mistakes or limitations or a tendency to blame:** Fear often places people on the defensive, making them unable to recognize or take responsibility for mistakes or acknowledge their own limitations. This fragility destroys the fluid interaction of a group that is necessary for success. An individual may even feign confidence or competence to prevent others from suspecting weakness.

- **Lack of humor, warmth, and confidence:** When people are afraid they stuff their emotions and begin to lose what makes them human. Once the human connection is lost, it is less likely for compassion and connection to be part of a group, which will make it more likely to become polarized over tough issues.
- **Lack of cooperation:** Fear of success or failure may cause people to behave and interact in counterproductive ways—often subconsciously—and undermine progress.

At this stage in the process of addressing fear dynamics, you do not need to identify the underlying cause of the fear. All you are looking for are symptoms indicating that something may be going on beneath the surface with one or more individuals in the group to explain the lack of progress or the counterproductive actions or interactions that are taking place.

Step 2: *Identify the General Source of the Fear*

The second step to managing fear dynamics is to identify the source of the fear. This recognition is important, as finding the source may help to determine whether your reaction to the situation is rational or irrational if you are working through the decision tree (Fear Dynamics Technique #5, page 71). Start by examining the following three areas from general to specific:

- **Cultural norms:** A growing area of research is in the sociology of fear—the study of what people in different cultures fear and to what degree. For example, in a study entitled "Cultural Aspects of Social Anxiety and Social

Anxiety Disorder," researchers Stefan G. Hofmann and Anu Asnaani of Boston University, along with Devon E. Hinton of Harvard University, examined the cultural aspects of social anxiety and social anxiety disorder (SAD) and found that social anxiety (the fear of negative evaluation by others) is more prevalent in Russia and the United States than it is in Asian cultures. A reasonable conclusion from this study is that one manifestation of fear is instilled by the cultural environment in which we are raised.

- **Localized norms:** By "localized," I mean smaller groups of people, such as a community, a business, or a family. These smaller groups may also operate within a culture of fear that influences the thoughts and behaviors of members of these social groups. For example, children often "inherit" fears from their parents, and people in businesses that nurture a culture of fear tend to be less innovative due to a fear of failure and the repercussions they are likely to suffer as a result.

- **Situational fear:** On an even smaller scale, fear can enter a relationship among two or more people involved in handling a given situation, such as a major (or even a minor) life decision, a family crisis, or a business deal. Even if only one individual in the pair or group is driven by fear, that fear impacts everyone in the group.

Keep in mind that fear can be productive or counterproductive. A single person in the group may perceive a threat that nobody else in the group is aware of, and that person may be able to steer the group clear of what would otherwise be a harmful outcome.

Some people, perhaps because of their culture or the way they were raised and educated, are better able than others to "sense" threats or analyze situations.

Step 3: *Identify the Specific Source of the Fear*

Fear is a feeling, a product of the mind. To identify the source of the fear, start by asking why the person or people are saying what they are saying or are behaving in a certain way. You likely need to ask this question of yourself and of the people who appear to be driven by fear. Continue to ask questions until you reveal the source of the person's fear or uncertainty.

> **Pro Tip:** In many cases, identifying the fear and its source is sufficient to overcome it.

I often find that when I call attention to the presence of fear in a business deal, for example, the person or people feeling the fear understand the motivation behind their thoughts and behaviors, can determine for themselves whether the fear is justified and helpful or not, and are able to make any adjustments necessary to handle the situation appropriately.

> *The process of trying to understand the fear dynamics can be helpful in itself.*

Note that this process assumes full access to information and that you are working in a cooperative group. In an ideal world, people would be open to discussions of fear and their behaviors in a group generally, but this is not an ideal world. An important aspect of this process is that, even if you can work through the process only internally with no cooperation from others in the dynamic, there is benefit to you because you will either identify some internal fear you have that is affecting the dynamic or, at a minimum, you will have gone through a thoughtful and reflective exercise to understand the other actors.

This process will reap rewards even if it is not a full resolution of the perceived issues. The process of trying to understand the fear dynamics can be helpful in itself.

Step 4: *Address the Source of the Fear*

The final step in the process of managing fear dynamics is to deal with the source of the fear. If the source is a very real threat the group will want to act on that threat. However, if the fear is unwarranted or excessive, the fear itself poses what could be described as a *lost opportunity threat*: the failure to take advantage of a potentially lucrative opportunity.

Pro Tip: Most importantly, never ignore irrational thoughts or behaviors in yourself or others, whatever their source. They will not go away, and they have the potential to lead to serious negative consequences.

Confront the behaviors, identify what is driving them, and address the source. As professor and author Joseph Campbell wrote, "The cave you fear to enter holds the treasure you seek."

Managing Fear Dynamics: In Review

- **Step 1:** Recognize the Symptoms of Fear Dynamics
- **Step 2:** Identify the General Source of the Fear
- **Step 3:** Identify the Specific Source of the Fear
- **Step 4:** Address the Source of the Fear

TACKLING FEAR DYNAMICS AT HOME AND AT WORK WITH RATIONAL DECISION-MAKING

Research shows that a high percentage of our choices are fear-based. Most of us base the vast majority of our decisions on what we believe to be the safest choice. We are afraid of the potential consequences of other choices that carry more perceived risk, even if data and logic indicate they are the better choices.

I cannot speak for anyone else, but for most of my life virtually all my decisions were fear-based (consciously or subconsciously). I chose to go to a state university (What if I don't get into an Ivy?), attended law school (How else could I earn a living?), and even got married the first time (Can I deal with being alone?) because these were the safe choices from an emotional standpoint.

In contrast, the rational decisions (the ones not based on fear) I made have had the best long-term outcomes. For instance, I moved from the comfort of a small law firm to a large national firm to grow my practice. I was able to make this decision even before I did a lot of the emotional work that I talk about in this book, because deep down I knew that it was the best decision for my family, even though I was petrified at the prospect of making a move with no clear path to gaining clients or developing my business.

In that same vein, we moved to a mountain community in the foothills of Denver over fifteen years ago, knowing it would be best for our family. If it were not for my wife and thinking about my son and the opportunity for him to grow up so close to nature, I suspect fear would have convinced me to stay put. Since then, I have progressed to being able to analyze my options and make choices driven not by fear but by facts supplemented by emotion. I wish I would have had my system in place back then because I would not have been so overwrought making these decisions. Fear limits choices while facts expand opportunities. Developing this skill has helped me immeasurably in my personal and professional life.

Making good decisions may involve some degree of intuition developed over the course of years of experience, but I do not propose that you rely solely on intuition or a nebulous Zen-like mystical force as your guide. The first step to making decisions *not* driven by fear is to question a decision driven primarily by emotion—emotion that may be rooted in falsehoods you came to accept over the course of your life. Among these falsehoods: you are not worthy of success, people cannot be trusted, and bad things are destined to happen to you.

> *Fear limits choices while facts expand opportunities.*

> *I have progressed to being able to analyze my options and make choices driven not by fear but by facts supplemented by emotion. Fear limits choices while facts expand opportunities.*

Sometimes the fear is simply the result of knowing that one path will be considerably more difficult than the other in the short term, and the potential benefits are too far into the future to see them clearly or understand or envision a path to success.

My Decision-Making System

A rational decision is one based on a combination of facts, logic, and desired outcomes *and* one that is free from the influence of anxiety and irrational fear. It is not necessarily the easy decision, although it certainly can be. To start changing my decision-making process, I examined my responses to situations to determine whether each response was irrational (based on fear and anxiety from my past) or rational (based on facts, logic, and desired outcomes in the present). From this examination, I developed a system for making rational, data-based decisions that I want to pass on to you. You can use this system for decision-making in your personal and professional life. I will give you examples from both arenas.

Step 1: *Breathe deeply and slowly*

When you feel fear, your natural inclination is to breathe rapidly and shallowly. Resist the urge by breathing deeply and slowly. Closing your eyes can help you focus on your breathing and take your mind off the source of your fear. Taking time to breathe may sound trite, but I have come to be a convert of this simple technique.

I consciously take a deep breath or two before a phone call that may be confrontational or when entering a room to start negotiations.

This is also an excellent time to utilize Fear Dynamics Technique #2 (page 31)and check in with your inner little guy. If this is a decision affecting your personal life there may be emotion surrounding it and doing a "gut check" will help you isolate what you may strongly want in this situation (although what you want doesn't necessarily mean it is the right choice).

Step 2: *Think*

Fear drives impulsivity in thought and action. You may feel the need to make a decision or fire off a response sooner than is necessary. Instead, spend some time analyzing the situation and thinking about the wisdom of the actions you are about to take or the words you are about to say or type. Try writing down what you are thinking at this moment. This will slow down your thinking and restrain your impulses. Of course you then need to resist the urge to share what you just wrote. Give yourself five minutes, an hour or two, or "sleep on it" to reflect and rethink when your mind is in a calmer state.

> **Pro Tip:** When you're anxious or angry, writing down what you are thinking and feeling is a great way to release the emotional pressure.

With all your thoughts and feelings on paper you don't have to worry about remembering them or following rabbit holes as your mind spins out of control, and you can examine them more objectively later.

> *I consciously take a deep breath or two before a phone call that may be confrontational or when entering a room to start negotiations.*

This step is also the right time to rely on Fear Dynamics Technique #5 (page 71) and create a decision tree. Make a list of pros and cons. Include both what you think and how you feel (emotional factors), along with objective facts and figures.

> **Pro Tip:** Be sure to factor in that the most challenging option may also present the greatest opportunities for growth, happiness, or level of success.

Analyze your decision tree and make a preliminary decision.

Step 3: *Give yourself more time*

Feeling bound by time to make a decision or take action can increase anxiety and impulsiveness. This is the time to use this technique and build in a pause (see Fear Dynamics Technique #4, page 48).

In a professional setting, deadlines are sometimes contrived or self-imposed, and they can almost always be pushed a bit or manipulated without risk to clients or the flow of a deal. You may have noticed that high-pressure sales pitches frequently give people very little time to decide. That is by design. The salespeople are working to create a fear of losing out on a great deal. This fear works to inhibit your brain's ability to think rationally.

I have often found that taking some extra time when engaged in a negotiation (a day when possible or even as little as five minutes when little time is available) gives all parties the confidence to move forward and feel better about the deal when they look back at it. I have found it to be a value-add to transactions—especially in crunch time at closing—if there is an acknowledgement to the parties that I, or my client, needs five to ten minutes to consider a point. I have even stated that we want to take the time to pause and make sure we understand our position and the dynamic in order to engage with the other side more productively. It may seem like a loss of flow or weakness, but usually these sorts of pauses actually add to overall efficiency and positive deal dynamics because it forces both sides, not just my side, to pause and think.

Step 4: *Gather information*

A great way to challenge your beliefs is to gather more information. If you have a concern about what you believe someone is thinking or has said, ask the person for clarification. For example, if you are worried about the ramifications of a clause in an agreement, work to understand the clause fully. Do your research to plug the gaps between certainty and uncertainty. By seeking out information in a pressured situation, you will force yourself to slow down, reflect on the situation, and figure out the question you want to ask.

Because the person with more information is likely your adversary, seeking more information will often create a more productive dynamic. You will understand the other person more and they will learn more about you. In addition, showing that you are willing to learn can often create a collaborative environment as people move to solve the problem rather than to win.

> *If you have a concern about what you believe someone is thinking or has said, ask the person for clarification.*

Gathering information will help you prevent fear and related anxiety from governing your choices in business, your workplace, or your personal life. Fear tends to lead to conflict, distrust, poor decisions, and irrational behaviors that impede productivity and undermine successful deals, as well as personal relationships.

Step 5: *Challenge your beliefs and ask yourself questions*

Fear is often triggered by false beliefs, bias, or misunderstandings that often are corrected by facts and clarification. Whenever you feel fear, frustration, or anger over something, ask yourself the following questions to determine whether you are reacting to a fact or a belief:

- If I make this choice, what is the worst that can happen?
- Analyze that "worst" outcome objectively by asking questions: How likely is it to occur; and if it does occur, what are the potential consequences? (This step is key to weighing the risk of the decision).
- Is what I fear based on fact or assumption (belief)?
- What is the source of the information or the creator of the pressure? Is it possible that this source is biased or has ulterior motives?
- What objective evidence and personal experience supports what I am thinking or have been led to believe?
- Am I assuming or do I know for sure?
- Is what I am thinking always true or only sometimes true?
- Am I making this better or worse in my mind than it really is?
- What facts do you need to change your mind or make you more confident to decide?
- How does this decision make me feel? Energized? Calm? Nervous? Heavy? The hope is that you have a positive feeling from the decision. If not, then you need to understand why you dread the choice or the likelihood and severity of the potential negative outcome. You may need to repeat this process several times to fully separate and examine all the issues you are battling.

This last bullet point requires that your final gut check gives you the positive feeling you need to make the choice. Note that the choice may still mean a tough road ahead, but that does not mean it is the wrong choice.

Step 6: *Act on your decision*

Act on your decision, confident in the fact that you carefully analyzed your options and their potential outcomes. Remember, regardless of the outcome, you made the right choice. Even good decisions can have negative outcomes, but even then, we can gain valuable knowledge, skills, and experience. Nothing ventured in life with eyes wide open is ever a total loss.

Let's look at an example of ordering lunch at a restaurant to see how you would use this six-step plan to rational decision-making. I can almost hear you scoff at this example, but earlier in my life a decision like this could cause vapor lock. It would go like this: I looked at the menu and narrowed it down to two choices: burger or Caesar salad. My entire body was crying out *Burger!* but then guilt and fear crept in. I had made a firm commitment to improving my health and fitness. I had these thoughts: "I really should order the Caesar salad. If I order the burger, I will have failed in my commitment to eating healthier." I felt embarrassed and ashamed I even considered the burger. Maybe (hopefully) you never went through this burger angst like me, but, regardless, the simple example is helpful to see how the steps work.

Now, when faced with a choice like this, I pause, breathe, and clear my mind. I take a few breaths and check in to see which option I'm leaning toward—definitely burger. I note my initial preference and move to the second step: an objective evaluation of the facts, the pros and cons. Of course, I am not suggesting that for every decision, like this burger versus salad one, you grab paper and pencil and sketch out a decision tree.

In this lunch scenario, I would formulate questions to examine the facts of the situation. For example, did I work out this morning? Was I going to have a small dinner? Does this restaurant have good burgers? Suppose I answer all those questions yes, then I would feel comfortable ordering the burger.

Next, I ask myself, "What is the worst possible outcome of this decision?" and I rationally analyze the likelihood of that possibility and what that reality would look like. For this burger choice, I might think, *Well, the worst outcome of this decision is that I'm going to feel too full to eat dinner.* Last, I check back in with my inner self, take a breath and see how this decision "feels" when I just take a moment and sit with it. If this decision makes me feel "good" (energized and excited or calm and resolute, depending on the situation), I am ready to move forward with the decision. In this example, I give a nod to the beef because the burger sounds great and the worst that can happen is that I'll have to skip dinner or eat light later.

Applying the System to More Complex Decisions

Now, consider applying this decision-making process to a more significant decision. For example, deciding whether to move to a new location. We recently moved to a different home and I relied on my rational decision-making process. First, check what your gut instinct is telling you. Maybe you just have an urge to move or you feel as though you need a change. Or maybe you've always fantasized about living in a particular place. Note the direction you are leaning, then move to the next step of analyzing your choices rationally.

Pro Tip: Make a list of pros and cons. In this case, the list could be long and varied and likely requires some additional research. Pros could range from the clearly objective (my family needs a bigger place) to the more emotional (I'm in a rut and need a change of scenery). Cons could also range from objective (if I were to sell now, I would have to sell at a loss) to emotional (I'll miss my neighbors).

With a decision like this, your list is definitely going to include an objective financial analysis, which may require help from a banker or other financial advisor. With a big decision, spend more time on your list.

Pro Tip: Research your pros and cons, get your team of experts to weigh in, brainstorm with other stakeholders. Sit with it. Share it with people who know you and with those you trust.

The purpose of this step in the decision-making process is to eliminate the unknowns, which create fear and anxiety. Facts shed light on your choices and often make one option stand out, almost making the decision for you.

When you have a clear preference, move to the next, scariest, step—the *what's the worst that can happen?* step. If you make this choice and follow this course of action, what is the worst possible outcome?

This step can really stir your pot of fears and anxiety. I am great at catastrophizing, and I usually advise against it, but at this stage in the process, I encourage it. Go ahead and dive down the worst-case-scenario rabbit hole. What is the one possible outcome that would keep you up at night? Are you worried that you might lose your job and not be able to afford the mortgage? Are you afraid you will lose touch with friends and family members? If you're struggling to come up with a worst-case scenario, ask yourself, "What's the one thing holding me back from making this choice?"

Be honest, you are in a judgment-free zone. When we recently moved, I realized the worst rational thing would be that we didn't like it and we could sell the house and move somewhere else. I would not lose my job, I would not be destitute. The catastrophic, irrational, outcomes would not actually occur.

> *I am great at catastrophizing, and I usually advise against it, but at this stage in the process, I encourage it. Go ahead and dive down the worst-case-scenario rabbit hole.*

After identifying one or more worst-case scenarios, you may want to update your pros and cons list and conduct additional research to examine the likelihood and severity of your worst-case scenarios. Consulting your team of experts and other stakeholders also is a great way to gather additional information and insight that sheds light on such questions as "Is this house too expensive for me?" and "Is my job unstable?"

When you examine these questions objectively, you gain a more rational perspective of what you consider is the worst possible outcome. You may find that your mind has blown it completely out of proportion and that if you were objectively advising someone in a similar situation, you would quickly dismiss the person's concern as trivial.

Suppose you complete the steps and conclude that the move would be affordable, the new location would be ideal, and your worst-case scenarios are highly unlikely to occur. (Of course, in 2019, most people never imagined the global pandemic and cultural and political upheaval in the US, but rational decisions need to be based on realistic probabilities, not fear-induced speculation.)

Do not forget the last step before you act on your decision:

- Check back in with your gut to see how this decision makes you feel.
- Pretend you made the decision to move.
- Are you excited about moving?
- Do you eagerly anticipate living in the new location?
- Are you comfortable with the decision?

If your answer to those questions is yes, then moving is the right decision. If, instead, you feel anxious, heavy, sad, and profoundly unsure, then staying put is the right decision. Yes, whatever you choose to do or not do is the right decision, as long as it is based on facts and arrived at through rational thought. If you move, you will be starting a new chapter in your life. If you stay, you will probably be more content with the status quo after having thoroughly (and rationally) examined your options.

The decision you make is secondary to knowing that you made a decision based on your reality and your wants and needs, not on fear and irrational thought. In addition, upon completing this process, you are stronger and better equipped to make decisions for yourself instead of being at the mercy of external circumstances or conditions and emotional baggage from the past.

What is most important is that you have a process in place that can assist you in making fact-based, rational decisions. This will make you happier in the long run.

Maintaining Composure Amid Chaos

The COVID-19 pandemic put my decision-making process to the test, as it did for most people. It has tested everyone's ability to make rational, data-based decisions. Leadership at all levels and around the world struggled, and they made wildly different decisions—some choosing to quarantine, others not; some choosing to mandate that masks be worn, and others not; some trusting certain medications, and others pursuing different ones.

During this time of uncertainty, I had bouts of feeling overwhelmed, and I sometimes felt on the edge of tumbling down a catastrophizing waterfall. What prevented me from backsliding into fear-and-anxiety-mode and helped me remain more proactive—as opposed to reactive—was having an infrastructure and system in place that enabled me to more effectively manage my thought process. When you backslide into reactive mode, you begin to feel as though you have no control, and when you lose control, fear and anxiety will skyrocket. That is a tough cycle to break if you do not have some system in place to maintain internal order.

What I find most striking about how people responded and still continue to respond to the pandemic is how reactive almost everyone is. At nearly every turn, there is confusion about which direction to take. The confusion and mixed messaging made it nearly impossible to make fact-based, rational decisions, because the "facts" were in a constant state of flux.

> *When you backslide into reactive mode, you begin to feel as though you have no control, and when you lose control, fear and anxiety will skyrocket.*

For several weeks I, like many of my colleagues, felt bombarded by client anxiety, and when I paused it became clear to me that fear and anxiety of the unknown were driving people's decision-making processes. Sadly, this reality continues to play out well after the pandemic.

What I found interesting as I worked to be an effective advisor to my clients, leader to my team, and a good friend and family member, is that my decision-making process worked even when worst-case scenarios were unfolding. I found comfort in that process. While the circumstances influencing my decisions had changed dramatically, the process continued to work. This allowed me to engage in a genuine and reflective manner with most people.

I admit that there were moments when I felt overwhelmed with the massive twists and turns that have become part of everyone's current existence, but I can also take a step back and see that I have been much more effective with my decision-making process in place than I ever could have been without it.

> *My decision-making process worked
> even when worst-case scenarios were
> unfolding. I found comfort in that process.
> While the circumstances influencing my
> decisions had changed dramatically,
> the process continued to work.*

I trust the process and I trust myself to work through it. The process has already proven itself time and time again in helping me make choices that delivered highly desirable outcomes. Nearly all the decisions I made by following the process worked out well for me in some fashion. Some of those decisions required action, others required only patience. As I have said to my clients and deeply believe myself, "Sometimes the best decision is no decision, and sometimes the best course of action is inaction."

As the pandemic has played out, I have worked with clients and colleagues to walk through some version of my decision-making process. I did not inform them prior to engaging in the process that we would be following a structured format, but during our discussions I subtly guided them through the process. I have led people down the pros and cons list and have spent quite a bit of time helping them identify and analyze their worst-case scenarios.

I find it fascinating that when people articulate their worst-case scenario, the specter of it is immediately diminished. Just putting it out there has a de-escalating effect. When the worst case is made clear and potentially real, people can focus on what they would do if it were to happen, which often leads them to think of ways that would mitigate the worst case in the unlikely event that it occurs. As soon as they know the risk and are prepared with a way to address it, they often feel free to move forward with the decision they were previously reluctant to make.

I want to be clear that the early days of the pandemic and the shutting down of the economy were ugly, and everyone (including me) felt gut-punched and reeled from the unknown. My brief description of how I was able to use my process to structure discussions and decision-making is not a claim that my process is a cure-all that delivers positive outcomes in all situations all the time or that it was able to keep everyone, including myself, calm and collected. Conditions were harsh for me, many of my clients, colleagues, and other people I know. The process does not prevent negative events from occurring or from having a devastating impact on people's lives.

What it has allowed me to do is to feel as though I have some control once I know the facts, even as the facts change. Even a modicum of control to latch onto at times was enough to allow calm and rational thought even in circumstances when facts were in doubt and reactivity and supposition ruled.

In many instances, no good options were available, only less bad ones. What my process allowed me to do was to think, act, and engage in discussions and problem-solving sessions with others knowing that the outcome of any decision would be negative. The ability to think and act, even when all decisions have painful consequences is key to ensuring that decisions are at least based on facts and a rational thought process that produce a plan of action.

Chapter 9

BALANCE FEAR AND TRUST

O ne outcome of my personal mental health journey is that it gave me greater insight into the role that emotions play in our professional lives—specifically, how recognizing the delicate balance between fear and trust can enlighten business relationships. It's true that as a corporate mergers and acquisitions (M&A) lawyer, I spend a large part of my time writing and reviewing contracts and advising clients on opportunities and risks, and on their legal rights, responsibilities, and obligations related to their business dealings. However, what is most fascinating about my job is observing and analyzing how emotions significantly impact business deals.

Often, these fear dynamics go unnoticed by the participants. While most participants consciously focus on price, timing, and other terms, their actions and decisions are actually often driven by emotion—fear, anger, expectation, hope, disappointment, and so on.

It's my opinion that fear, trust, and the interaction and balance between the two emotions have the most impact in work relationships or business deals. Frankly, I don't know which is scarier because either emotion of fear or trust can make people act irrationally. Acting out of fear, a participant is likely to overreact to a perceived threat in the negotiation or overanalyze an agreement to the point of losing out on a potentially good deal. On the other hand, participants who are overly trusting may enter into an agreement without carefully thinking it through and later regret their decision.

A healthy balance of fear and trust leads to better outcomes. The trick is creating and maintaining that balance.

Fear as Business Friction

Business friction is anything that blocks progress, impairs productivity, or slows the pace of innovation and business itself. In physics, friction is the resistance that one object or surface encounters when rubbing against or moving over another object or surface. In a car, friction between the many moving parts reduces fuel efficiency. Energy needed to move the vehicle is partially used to overcome friction and is lost in the form of heat. Friction and the resulting heat cause wear and tear on components that eventually results in the need for repairs.

> *A healthy balance of fear and trust leads to better outcomes. The trick is creating and maintaining that balance.*

In a business, friction results in a loss of focus, creativity, confidence, and direction, and negatively impacts productivity and achievement. Moreover, organizational friction inhibits innovation, which often results in decreased sales, poor client and talent retention, and the inability to act nimbly to take advantage of opportunities. All of these make a business less efficient and therefore less productive. Secondary effects of business friction may be negative cultural changes, personal and business stagnation, and a lack of accountability.

A significant source of business friction—but one that is rarely discussed openly—is fear, which negatively impacts action, interaction, and transaction. In business, fear discourages people from taking initiative, challenging the status quo, forming partnerships, exploring opportunities, and making deals. Fear can create a lackadaisical workforce with no personal investment in the business or vision—people just going through the motions and not being invested in the outcomes. This is a recipe for disaster.

Fear creates friction. How can it not? If employees are afraid to point out problems or are afraid of having their ideas shot down, opportunities are lost. If a customer service representative is afraid to negotiate and engage with customers, how effective will that person be in improving customer satisfaction? If leadership is paranoid, how effective will it be in pursuing partnerships and making decisions to improve the company?

Using Fear to Your Advantage

Keep in mind that fear is not necessarily always counterproductive. Major decisions and initiatives should be approached with some degree of fear and apprehension. Fear is what motivates people to perform their due diligence—challenging their beliefs and gathering more information to confirm or lessen those fears. Fear makes people more vigilant, so they proceed more cautiously and carefully. Rational fear can sharpen both your focus and critical thinking to identify issues that need to be addressed.

Problems arise when fear results in tunnel vision and triggers physiological reactions that eclipse rational thought. As part of our body's fear response, the brain's amygdala signals the adrenal gland to release stress hormones, including adrenaline and cortisol, which can inhibit complex decision-making and memory, as well as our ability to communicate effectively—the exact qualities you want to have in full functional mode when looking at an important business decision.

When confronted by fear, we tend to see issues in black and white and may be unable to grasp the overall picture and nuance in a situation. For example, in a business deal, we may focus almost exclusively on a single issue (for example, a closing date) that presses one of our buttons, while losing sight of other issues that have a potentially greater impact (positive or negative).

To use fear to your advantage, look at it as a canary in a coal mine—an early warning signal that something may not be right—but pause before acting on your initial reaction on that fear. Instead of fighting, fleeing, or freezing in fear, gather the courage to confront your fear and examine it more closely. As Nelson Mandela once said, "Courage does not mean the absence of fear, but the triumph over it."

> *To use fear to your advantage, look at it as a canary in a coal mine—an early warning signal that something may not be right.*

Using Fear Dynamics Technique #9 (page 161), the goal is to shift from fear (emotional response) to analysis (rational thought) to figure out the basis of your "gut" or "primitive" reaction. The presence of fear is a signal to slow down, pay attention, and work through what you are experiencing to give yourself the best chance to act thoughtfully and not reactively.

Leveraging Trust to Reduce Business Friction

In business, trust is a currency. As Stephen M.R. Covey points out in his book *The Speed of Trust*, trust reduces friction in business, increasing speed while reducing costs. Covey uses the analogy of airport security after 9/11 to illustrate his point. After the terrorist attacks on the World Trade Center in Lower Manhattan, trust at airports in the US was at an all-time low. As a result, increased security at checkpoints resulted in longer waits and higher costs. I see the same pattern in business deals. When I help clients who have a well-established, trusting relationship with their counterparty navigate a business transaction, the deal proceeds much faster and at a lower cost than do transactions between individuals who barely know one another.

When two parties begin a negotiation, they have a shared trust account that contains a small amount of this currency. (Unless we have reason to distrust a person, we generally trust most people initially.) As both parties proceed in the negotiation they contribute to or withdraw from that shared trust account.

A good approach to negotiation is to keep an eye on the "balance" in the shared trust account and conduct yourself in a way that contributes to the account while monitoring other factors that contribute to or withdraw from that account. For example, you may be able to point out how your interests align, work toward improving transparency, or ask questions to root out the source of the other party's apparent distrust or reticence to moving forward with you.

> *Building a culture of trust encourages sharing, collaboration, and innovation within a company.*

Using trust to reduce business friction can be extended from deals and negotiations to business functions and operations across a company. For example, building a culture of trust encourages sharing, collaboration, and innovation within a company. In contrast, a culture in which coworkers are competing against one another for raises, promotions, and acknowledgement breeds a culture of fear (and a lack of trust) that discourages sharing and collaboration.

You do not have to be an M&A attorney (or any kind of attorney) to use these tools of balancing fear and trust in your own professional world. I encourage you to take these lessons, including building in a pause and the decision-tree analysis, into your work world. For me, accepting that you cannot cleanly divide your life into your personal life and your professional life was integral to developing an encompassing, healthy perspective on living a happy life. Managing your emotions doesn't follow a nine-to-five clock. It's all life. I hope these techniques help you live yours in a happier way than you were before reading this book.

MAKING BIG CHANGES WITH TINY HABITS

One tool of change that I rely on is the "tiny habit." Whenever you make a commitment to any sort of self-improvement program, my advice is to take an incremental approach by adopting tiny habits—easy, routine thoughts or behaviors that you build on over time. Tiny habits are especially effective when attempting to change deeply entrenched thinking and behavioral patterns because you must unlearn what is already in place while developing and integrating new, healthier patterns.

Think of a big life change as an ocean voyage. Your ship is off course, but you do not need to make a sudden big change in direction to reach your destination. Steering the ship a few degrees north or south will have a huge impact on where it ends up over the course of a couple of thousand miles. Likewise, making small adjustments—such as learning to build in a pause or using a decision tree—can dramatically improve your life over months or years of practice.

On the other hand, if you try to achieve major change over a short period of time, you are more likely to become frustrated and discouraged at the lack of progress you're making towards your goal, and you may even give up trying.

For example, if you decide to start a strength-building program by doing fifty push-ups every morning when you haven't done a single push-up in the last ten years, you're likely to fail on your first attempt and become discouraged. However, if you start with five push-ups and increase it by two push-ups every week or every month, you can more realistically work up to doing fifty push-ups every morning (maybe broken into five sets of ten each).

> *Making small adjustments—such as learning to build in a pause or using a decision tree—can dramatically improve your life over months or years of practice.*

I did not invent this concept of self-transformation through incremental change. Years ago, my wife, Libby, attended a conference at her alma mater and heard a talk by BJ Fogg, PhD, Director of the Behavior Design Lab at Stanford University. This talk focused on how creating a small daily change in your life can take root and make a substantial difference.

This tiny-habit concept really works. For example, my wife started getting terrible tension headaches from TMJ. To reduce their frequency and severity, she started doing three simple isometric head and neck exercises whenever she brushed her teeth in the morning. Then she added doing them after getting out of the shower and then when brushing her teeth at night. Since adopting this habit, she has had significantly fewer problems with headaches of any kind.

Likewise, our son repeated an affirmation to himself in the mirror every time he washed his hands. Often it was a skill he was trying to develop, such as calming down before a tennis match or test ("I calm myself down and perform at my highest level."). These affirmations have done wonders to help him achieve his goals, whatever they may be. An example of how I utilize tiny habits is to take a breath before I answer the phone. This reminds me to slow myself down.

The key is to make a small change that you can reliably perform routinely. When I made my commitment to stop letting fear and anxiety govern my life, I started slowly. First, I worked on building in a pause before responding to someone or reacting in situations. I started building in a pause during casual (non-stressful, non-confrontational) interactions. For example, pausing before answering the question of whether I would like fries or coleslaw with my BBQ sandwich. I worked on that until I felt comfortable and confident. Then, I started to transfer that same skill to more challenging interactions and situations, such as driving in heavy traffic. I practiced with friends and loved ones, and then moved up to using the technique with clients and colleagues in workplace interactions. My confidence and comfort level increased to the point at which I was able to use the technique during pressure-packed, multi-million-dollar transaction negotiations.

> *The key is to make a small change that you can reliably perform routinely. When I made my commitment to stop letting fear and anxiety govern my life, I started slowly.*

The tiny-habit approach is very effective. The goal is to start small with something that you can reliably perform with success and grow it into a game changer.

> **Pro Tip:** For more information on this approach to making major changes, I highly recommend Professor BJ Fogg's book, *Tiny Habits: The Small Changes That Change Everything.*

TRAIN YOUR BRAIN

When I returned to therapy in 2009, I was determined to make lasting changes. Frankly, I was desperate. I saw this wonderful life I had created with this beautiful little family slipping away from me. I knew I had to make real, foundational changes to the way I saw the world and reacted to it so I could stay with my family. Glossing over issues with a superficial mental-health cleanse was not going to work anymore.

Initially, I hoped my therapist would agree that I could go away to some kind of emotional "rehab" to escape the daily pain I felt interacting with my family, the world, and dealing with work pressures. However, she was adamant that part of the process was creating an integrated existence in actual living reality while simultaneously working on my issues. Highly motivated, I bought into her plan and committed to seeing her multiple times a week.

I'm not going to sugarcoat it. It was difficult and slow-going at first. The Fear Dynamics Techniques I've laid out for you in previous chapters were the result of many months, maybe even years, of hard work. My hope is that my process of self-discovery will help you shorten your process by providing you with hope and a framework to use to handle your fear and anxiety, regardless of the source.

One fact that I learned is the power of the human brain should not be underestimated. When fear and anxiety have you in their grip, your brain can be your most ferocious enemy or your most powerful ally. It can calm the fear and anxiety or magnify it exponentially in a vicious vortex that sucks you into the depths of despair. Fortunately, the brain has a greater capacity for change than most people realize. Thanks to neurogenesis and neuroplasticity, it also can grow new neurons (*neurogenesis*) and undergo structural or physiological changes (*neuroplasticity*) to develop new skills and new ways of thinking, even as an adult. In other words, you can train your brain just as you can build muscle through weight training and enhance heart and lung efficiency through cardiovascular exercise.

> *The power of the human brain should not be underestimated. When fear and anxiety have you in their grip, your brain can be your most ferocious enemy or your most powerful ally. Fortunately, the brain has a greater capacity for change than most people realize.*

As you learn a new skill, the brain changes. It develops new connections between neurons and may even grow new neurons to build even more connections. All you notice is that the more you practice, the better you get. You probably never realized that the reason you are improving is that your brain is changing through the development of these new communication pathways. Over time, the communication pathways are so entrenched and finely tuned that you can perform the skill almost without thinking. For example, when you walk across a room all you have to think about is where you want to go; your brain and body work out all the details subconsciously to get you there. However, learning to walk is a huge challenge requiring a great deal of practice. The entire time you were learning to walk your brain was creating the communication pathways needed to coordinate your movements.

When someone tells you that your anxiety or your sadness is "all in your head," in some ways they are correct. Over the course of your life, the brain has developed pathways to facilitate certain thought patterns. For example, if you tend to catastrophize, your brain creates pathways that support your ability to catastrophize. Even though it is a counterproductive and harmful habit the repetition leads to the creation of the pathways that facilitate that skill. Likewise, if you constantly feel threatened your brain builds pathways to make you hypersensitive and more reactive. Unfortunately, that makes you feel constantly on edge and anxious.

Someone once explained to me that brain pathways (neural connections) are like roads. If, as you are growing up, you respond to perceived threats by disconnecting, your brain creates a superhighway, increasing the speed and efficiency of that response. It becomes quick, easy, and familiar. In contrast, the desired response of thoughtful reflection in the face of a threat, which wasn't developed or fostered by caregivers in youth, is like a tiny dirt path that has become overgrown from a lack of use and maintenance.

The good news is that the brain is trainable. You can bulldoze that superhighway and build your own neural superhighways to facilitate desired thought patterns and responses. You can train your brain to process in more positive, healthier ways.

Without training, the adult brain follows the same thought patterns as those established in childhood. We all know people who have never grown up; their mental or emotional development stopped sometime in their past, maybe as long ago as their early teens. My emotional growth was stunted by the neglect and abuse from my parents and over the years I subconsciously reinforced those early pathways. I developed a superhighway of disconnectedness as that was an accessible initial path to escape the abuse and neglect of my childhood.

> *Over the course of your life, the brain has developed pathways to facilitate certain thought patterns.*
>
> *The good news is that the brain is trainable.*

I was able to access this more and more easily each year that passed. I had a tiny dirt path where productive and rational responses to conflict were found, but never used because the path was forgotten and never traveled. Only after I retrained my brain was I able to develop healthier and more mature paths in stressful situations.

Any thought patterns and responses ingrained in childhood are likely limited in their effectiveness to you as an adult. At the time of your development you did not have access to the full range of internal and external resources to effectively navigate through certain situations or deal with adult issues. The brain uses whatever tools available, and until it learns otherwise it continues to use these tools to respond, even though situations and issues become more complex and nuanced later in life and more effective tools become available.

As babies we cry to have our needs met, then we use words, then logic. In the same way, as we develop as adults we acquire more sophisticated tools to navigate and cope with reality—tools we acquire from books, therapy, observations, advice, experiences, and more.

Once I discovered that I could retrain my brain to respond in a certain way I began looking into different types of brain-training. I'm going to save you all the time and research that I put in to learn about how to train your brain to work for you instead of against you. This chapter discusses several brain-training methods you may want to consider.

I encourage you to explore each of these and find methods that work for you to develop more effective ways to process information, make decisions, solve problems, resolve conflict, and communicate. For me, the methods I describe in the following sections led to a foundational change in my happiness and ability to handle life's stressors.

Cognitive Behavioral Therapy (CBT)

Cognitive behavioral therapy (CBT) is a practical approach to retraining the brain by changing thought and behavioral patterns. It is commonly used in the treatment of depression and anxiety disorders. For example, if a client is feeling anxious the therapist and client work closely together to identify the source of that anxiety and challenge that source by analyzing it closely.

If the source of the anxiety is anticipation that some painful event will occur, such as the person's partner leaving the relationship, the therapist will challenge the client by asking (for example) how likely this is to occur, what evidence the client has to support this suspicion, and whether the client has tried to gather any additional information to confirm or support the suspicion. In other words, the therapist helps the client figure out whether the perceived threat is real or imagined.

> *The therapist trains the client to question and analyze their thought and behavior patterns on their own to develop more realistic perceptions and beliefs about themselves and others and about the world around them.*

Likewise, if the client is worried about losing his job, the therapist may ask how likely that is and why the client thinks it is likely to happen. If the client responds by saying something like, "My supervisor is always annoyed with me," the therapist may ask whether it's possible that something else is going on with the supervisor that is making her feel annoyed or frustrated. Or the therapist may ask the client to describe an incident in which the supervisor became annoyed and then lead the client through an analysis of that situation that may reveal that the client had nothing to do with making the supervisor annoyed.

Over time, the therapist trains the client to question and analyze their thought and behavior patterns on their own to develop more realistic perceptions and beliefs about themselves and others and about the world around them. While this process is very similar to Fear Dynamics Technique #8: Don't Be a Duck (page 137), there is a material difference in that a large piece of CBT is examining behavior that you want to engage in and foster in different situations and understanding what certain behaviors are not healthy for you in your situation.

Fear Dynamics Technique #8 and CBT are certainly related, but address different aspects of behavior observation and ultimately behavior choices. I believe that CBT is very useful as a basis to engage in technique #8 and avoid being like a duck. The goal is to help the client develop a more analytical mind that welcomes objective analysis of the environment and an internal dialogue that results in a clearer, fact-based understanding.

CBT can start to work over a relatively short period of time (twenty weeks or so), but the benefits are not lasting without ongoing efforts to maintain the changes in thought and behavioral patterns and underlying neural pathways. Some form of long-term psychotherapy, such as the next four therapies I describe, are useful for this purpose.

Relational Therapy

Relational therapy is a type of psychotherapy (talk therapy) that helps people build and maintain mutually satisfying relationships. While CBT helped me deal effectively with acute (short-term) reactions and interactions, relational therapy targeted chronic (long-term) underlying issues. CBT is great for treating symptoms, while relational therapy identifies and addresses underlying causes and how they are rooted in past experiences.

For example, in my situation, CBT helped me develop coping strategies to certain triggers (*i.e., my overreaction to being criticized*). Relational therapy delves into the source of those triggers (*i.e., my dad constantly belittled me throughout my life*). As previously described, one of my core issues was fear of authority and being found out as a fraud. Anxiety pervaded this mindset. In working to understand the core cause of this self-belief, I was able to then recognize the irrational reaction I was having as an adult to perceived issues others had with me.

The process involves building a strong relationship with the therapist so underlying issues can be exposed and discussed in the context of an actual relationship that is safe. This process shifts the focus from changing the behavior or reaction to understanding the underlying dysfunction—when, how, and why it developed.

This deep understanding and the resulting personal development cannot be achieved in a vacuum—it must be done in a relationship with another person. The behavior was learned through a relationship—in my case, predominately with the relationships with my parents. So, in order to learn a different narrative, the work needs to be done relationally with another person for it to be the most effective.

> *This deep understanding and the resulting personal development cannot be achieved in a vacuum—it must be done in a relationship with another person.*

Neurofeedback

Neurofeedback is a form of biofeedback. Biofeedback is a type of mind-body technique that trains people to improve their health by controlling certain bodily processes that normally happen involuntarily, such as heart rate, and blood pressure. These automatic bodily functions are electronically monitored and then this information is used to help control the function, (*i.e., lower your heart rate*). Specifically, neurofeedback means engaging with your brain waves. The person engaged in a neurofeedback session receives positive feedback for the desired brain activity and negative feedback for the undesirable brain activity.

In a typical session, after being connected to a brain wave monitor that is set to encourage certain brain waves the patient will watch a video like a movie or a TV show. When the brain waves are in the desired range, the video and audio are clear. When the brain waves fall out of the desired range, the audio and video become silent and dark. Your brain wants to see the movie so it corrects itself to have the desired brain wave activity. I explain my personal experience in more detail below.

I first found out about neurofeedback when my therapist suggested I might benefit from some neuroscience work as part of my relational therapy. She believed my brain was not working as efficiently as it could when it was in certain emotional states. I had difficulty taking a deep dive into certain topics that triggered a strong emotional response because my brain remembered the pain and worked hard to avoid feeling that pain again, thus avoiding the conversation. This can manifest in the brain working too fast or slowing down, either of which becomes a significant block to working through difficult issues.

Neurofeedback can train the brain to be less reactive and more fluid. It sounded a little nutty to me years ago but now it is fairly commonplace. I recently watched *Quarterback* on Netflix and saw Minnesota Vikings quarterback Kirk Cousins using neurofeedback to train his brain to stay calm during tense moments in a football game.

The first step in neurofeedback therapy is to create a brain map to diagnose anomalies in brain activity. I had to wear a cap with sensors for measuring brain waves. Based on the brain map the therapist designs a program to train the brain to operate more efficiently and bring the various brain waves into optimal ranges.

My training involved wearing the brain-wave-sensor cap while watching a movie. When my brain waves were in the desired range, the image on the screen remained steady, but when my brain waves wandered outside the desired range, the image would shake, and the sound would cut out for a moment. Subconsciously, the brain works to maintain stable sound and video.

Neurofeedback helped me engage with my memories and the current triggers in my life that bring the emotions of those memories roaring to the surface more effectively without becoming overwhelmed and slowing my brain down or following counterproductive pathways. It helped me stay connected in difficult conversations and engage more clearly. It accelerated my ability to work through stubborn issues by training my brain to remain in the moment.

> *Neurofeedback can train the brain to be less reactive and more fluid.*

When I first mention neurofeedback to people, many of them wonder whether it is a form of mind control or brainwashing. It is not. It is more like a brain tune-up that improves brain function. You could compare it to a getting an adjustment from a chiropractor to ensure that your bones are aligned before engaging in a fitness program. It is not a quick-fix procedure that restructures how you think and behave, it simply helps the brain function more effectively and efficiently so that the serious work of psychotherapy can produce the desired results. Look at it in terms of a fitness program.

If you've been sedentary for the past five years, you probably shouldn't wake up one day, lace up your running shoes, and head out for a ten-mile run. Instead, you should get a physical first and address any underlying conditions that might negatively affect your ability to exercise.

> *When I first mention neurofeedback to people, many of them wonder whether it is a form of mind control or brainwashing. It is not.*

Just as proper medical treatment enables you to engage in a fitness program, neurofeedback enables your brain to engage in psychotherapy and get the most out of it. You do not have to be in therapy to benefit from neurofeedback; it can help with maintaining focus or even with sleep. It enables optimal processing of information and inputs so that you can engage thoughtfully and rationally with the world. Brain training is an effective tool for almost anyone. Our son was diagnosed with ADHD in middle school and neurofeedback helped him train his brain to maintain focus and concentration during tests. My wife has also used it to help her maintain focus on demanding mental tasks.

I can tell the difference. It's fascinating. I remember one afternoon, getting on a plane from Miami to Denver, I was exhausted and looking forward to the quiet of the plane and limited interruptions from email and phone calls. As the plane took off a little girl in the row behind me began crying loudly. In the past, this situation would have made me extremely agitated. Instead, this time I had a more reflective and empathetic reaction. I felt bad for the parents who obviously did not want their child to be screaming. I was able to take the sensory onslaught and frustration and not let it sit and simmer with me. I calmly put on my headphones, turned on my meditation soundtrack, and settled in for the flight. I breathed calmly and my thoughts were rational. Before I knew it the girl had stopped crying and had fallen asleep and I was able to remain relaxed throughout the flight.

> *Neurofeedback enables optimal processing of information and inputs so that you can engage thoughtfully and rationally with the world.*

Holosync Meditation Technology

Holosync meditation involves listening to nature sounds that contain soundwaves at frequencies outside the range of human hearing. These frequencies stimulate a part of each brain hemisphere (left and right) called the *olivary nucleus* to create new neural pathways that connect the two hemispheres, thereby enabling whole-brain thinking. It combines brain training with meditation, essentially delivering the benefits of both in an accelerated fashion.

I use it to help reduce anxiety and to help me engage in the world more thoughtfully and reflectively. I simply download the soundtracks onto my iPhone and listen to them on my headphones during the day at home and work. When I listen at work I leave my office and the related distractions, go to a conference room, put on my headphones, and listen in a calm, meditative state.

When I started with holosync meditation I wondered what others would think if they saw me practicing meditation. Most people were curious, and several have adopted the practice to the point at which they routinely engage the meditative mind when situations call for it.

Mindfulness Meditation

Mindfulness meditation involves bringing your full attention into the moment, "the now," so that you can acknowledge and accept your thoughts, feelings, and sensations without judgment. If you think about it, most of what makes us anxious and afraid is not real. It is not part of what we are dealing with in the here and now. It is either in the past (no longer posing a threat) or in the future (has not happened yet and may never happen). Yet what we most worry about are events in the past or the bad that *might* happen in the future. By bringing our full attention to the present we neutralize the past and future so that it has no power over what we think or how we feel. Mindfulness meditation calms the mind and body, slows down racing thoughts, and allows us to let go of any negativity.

> By bringing our full attention to the present we neutralize the past and future so that it has no power over what we think or how we feel.

Think back to the most joyful times of your life. Chances are good that during those times you were totally engrossed in what you were doing, so focused on what you were doing in that very moment that there was no space for a thought about the past or a worry about the future to creep in. You were living in the moment and loving it. When I meditate, I sometimes focus on a beach trip that I recently took with my family. I feel the soft sand under my feet and I can hear the waves rhythmically rolling into the shore. I see the sun glinting off the water as my son and I set out on a kayak.

The core feeling is one of feeling connected and accepted in those moments, feeling the emotional content in those memories. Or you can think about an activity in which you were recently engaged at home or at work that required your total concentration. You probably felt pretty great doing it because you were so immersed in the activity that you completely blocked out everything else—any aches and pains, feelings about hating your job, worries about keeping your job or paying the mortgage, regrets about missed opportunities, thoughts about the world's injustices, anxieties related to current events, and so on.

Sometimes I will imagine myself on a run and feel the pounding of each step and my steady breath. When you are totally in the moment, you are in the zone, and you are not even aware of yourself as being separate from what's around you. *That* is an incredible feeling, and it is the feeling you want to re-create through mindfulness meditation.

Pro Tip: Practicing mindfulness meditation is very doable. Sequester yourself in a quiet place that will be free of distractions and interruptions for a certain period. It can be five minutes, ten minutes, or more. During that time relax, close your eyes, and immerse yourself in the present. Focus on your breathing and on physical sensations—sounds, scents, the feel of your clothes against your skin, your heartbeat. If your mind wanders, that's okay, just observe the thought or emotion as though it is a passing cloud (don't try to suppress it or ignore it), then return to the present by focusing on your breathing. There are any number of guides, apps, or articles that focus on mindful meditation. Find one that feels right for you and practice.

When you are totally in the moment, you are in the zone, and you are not even aware of yourself as being separate from what's around you. That is an incredible feeling.

As you progress in your mindfulness training try to integrate mindfulness throughout your personal and professional life and in all thought and action. If you are at work and your mind begins to wander, note where your mind has gone, then bring your thoughts back to the present. If you are at home spending time with loved ones and you notice your mind drifting to worries about work or something else that prevents you from being present in the company of the people you love, note the thought or concern and then bring your focus back to the here and now. As this practice becomes second nature you will begin to notice that you are living more and more fully in the present and drifting less and less into the past and future where fear and anxiety reign.

Positive Affirmations

Another brain training exercise I practice involves the daily repetition of positive affirmations—a practice popularized in the 19th century as part of the New Thought movement. The idea behind positive affirmations is that everything humans do and create begins with a thought or idea. To be, do, or have what you desire, you must imagine it first and sow the seeds of what you envision into your subconscious through the repetition of positive affirmations.

For example, if you decide you want to be able to build a table and say to yourself, "I'll never be able to figure out how to do that" or "I don't have the time or skill to build that," the negative thought becomes self-defeating, ensuring that your mind will never engage in the thinking necessary to obtain the skill and craft you desire. Only by believing that you can obtain what you desire or achieve a particular goal will your mind start working to figure out a way to make it happen.

I use positive affirmations to counteract the negative self-talk and falsehoods instilled in me during my childhood—the feelings that I don't matter, that I am a disappointment, that I am undeserving, and so on. When I look in a mirror (for example when washing my hands), I will take a few seconds and repeat a brief, positive affirmation, such as:

- My life is secure
- I am doing my best
- I achieve my goals
- My family is healthy, happy, and strong
- I am successful in my career and building on my success every day
- I am a good person
- My past does not define me

I strongly encourage you to make a habit of repeating positive affirmations. Although they may sound corny and were even satirized by Al Franken on Saturday Night Live's "Daily Affirmations with Stuart Smalley," the repetition of daily affirmations works wonders to correct self-defeating thoughts and prevent self-fulfilling prophecies.

Just think about it for a minute: Everything you do starts with a thought. If those thoughts are negative and you constantly feel disheartened, how can you possibly accomplish anything? As a youth, I was so mired in negative thinking I didn't consider pursuing activities that were not generally accepted. I only pursued them if they were easy and safe. Now, I am certain that positive affirmations have helped me achieve the level of success I have in business by bolstering my courage to take risks, follow my gut, and seek out rewards.

> *Just think about it for a minute:*
> *Everything you do starts with a thought.*
> *If those thoughts are negative and you*
> *constantly feel disheartened, how can*
> *you possibly accomplish anything?*

Discovering that I could train my brain liberated me from thinking that my past defined me or that my parents had ruined my life or destroyed me. For so long I felt broken, and I defined myself as permanently damaged, living without hope. Certainly my parents stunted my emotional development and damaged me psychologically, but thanks to neurogenesis and neuroplasticity I have the power to reshape my mind and my thought and behavioral patterns. In so doing, I have the power to overcome my past and define my destiny. You too have this power. Regardless of where you are on your own personal journey to happiness and self-fulfillment, I suggest trying some form of brain-training.

In the past I was afraid of voicing my opinions or speaking in public about what I had learned and knew about the M&A work I do. I had ideas about best practices and how to navigate difficult issues but would only think them and only share them with clients occasionally.

> *I have the power to overcome my*
> *past and define my destiny.*

Now, my default reaction to a challenge is not to doubt my ability or creativity, but to instead tackle the challenge with excitement and talk to people, even a large group, about what I have learned and how I have used the knowledge in real life situations. I am more energized about my skills and opportunities and that energy impacts my teammates and clients in a positive way as we work on various projects.

Chapter 10 ▶

MEMORIES AND THE FUTURE

We moved to a new house several years ago, which entailed the painstaking task of going through everything we owned and determining what to keep and what to toss. In the corner of the basement, I saw one tattered box with "ShopKo" barely still visible written in red lettering and opened it to find baseball trophies and plaques from my childhood.

I hadn't thought about playing baseball for years. I loved it when I was a kid. The first time I played on an actual team I was nine years old. I was lucky that my first season we had a good team; we won the league championship that year. But my favorite memories are of hanging out with my teammates.

After each game we had a parent-provided snack (Jolly Good soda and mini bags of Fritos were the usual fare back in my day). I liked the snack, but even more than that I was part of something bigger than myself, and I could be myself (or at least as close to myself as possible) around my teammates. Because I was only nine at least one of my parents would show up for a game. They set up camp in folding lawn chairs away from the bleachers and the other parents. I always dreaded the end of the post-game revelry when families filed back to their cars for the night. The freedom, easy times, and lightness of my hours with the team were over until the next game.

Summer baseball was a great escape from my home life—a chance to be just a kid running around outside in the sun, laughing with my friends. I felt sad every year when the end of August arrived and baseball season was over. When I was looking over my trophies and plaques all those years later, I let myself experience the feelings of accomplishment, belonging, and just plain fun I had playing baseball. For so many years I tried to erase and avoid all memories of my childhood. I believed there was nothing good back there, and, moreover, I was too afraid to closely examine my past because it was littered with too many painful landmines. It was easier to avoid it all, even at the cost of blotting out the good.

Embracing My Past

In that moment, I may not have been ready to embrace all the parts of my childhood, but I definitely did not want to forget them all either. I wouldn't have hauled around this box of memories for the last thirty-five years over countless moves if I truly wanted to completely forget my past.

We all have unique pieces of our past that link to our future selves. For many of us, parts of our past are so painful we keep them under lock and key, either consciously or subconsciously. I dreaded the thought of looking back at my past because it always led to overwhelming and crippling feelings of shame, loneliness, and fear, which then translated to anxiety. I made the decision that it was easier to erase it and disown it. It was all useless baggage—or so I thought.

Since then, I've come to realize the necessity of at least trying to understand my past and myself in order to live a happy, fulfilling life, *especially* because some aspects of my past were so painful. My gut instinct was to bury my memories of the past even though the only way to neutralize their negative power was to dig up, and dive into, those memories.

The prospect of delving into my past was terrifying. What helped me immensely was to examine my past objectively, as a disinterested third party. Sometimes I would approach the task as if I were a reader of someone else's story, so I would not get lost in the emotions and completely bail on the process. This was not, and is not, an easy exercise, but it helped me realize that some of the qualities I value in myself now were actually forged through the difficulties of my childhood.

> *I've come to realize the necessity of at least trying to understand my past and myself in order to live a happy, fulfilling life, especially because some aspects of my past were so painful.*

I know it may sound far-fetched, but through this process I learned to embrace the notion that even though many parts of my past are shameful, hurtful, or scary, I cannot change it. However,

I can discover some good qualities in myself that developed due to the difficulties of my childhood. For example, I work hard, am laser-focused, and have achieved financial security. I can now see that these qualities and achievement are directly related to what I learned and experienced, and what motivated me, during my difficult childhood.

Growing up I did not feel valued, respected, or even loved. By the time I was in seventh grade I realized nobody was stepping up to help me succeed in the world. My parents appeared to view me as an accessory in the stories they told others, not a stand-alone person to be valued and supported. I needed to prepare myself to get by in this world completely on my own. I needed to become self-reliant.

> *I can discover some good qualities in myself that developed due to the difficulties of my childhood.*

The biggest component to survival in my teenage mind was money. My first job (other than mowing neighbors' lawns) was shearing Christmas trees the summer I was thirteen. It was back-breaking work and I was the only teenager out in the fields.

Beginning that summer and over the next ten years I worked numerous jobs (bus boy, dishwasher, grocery bagger, dorm janitor, fry cook). I was not saving for an item or a trip. I just wanted to have money to do what I needed and wanted to do, and not have to ask for money from my parents or anyone . . . *ever*. This drive to work and save money came from a deep feeling of insecurity and aloneness in the world, but it produced something of value—a strong work ethic.

As I grew up, I continued to work hard in college, then law school, and over the years I built a successful law practice. To accomplish this, I relied on my work ethic and unflinching focus, both of which were born in me out of fear (almost terror) of abandonment and profound insecurity. My younger self constantly felt that at any moment whatever security was available would disappear in an instant. Whatever use I was to my parents would vanish, and they would move on without me. The irony of these anxieties is that is exactly what happened. Soon after I left for college, they divorced, and we all went our separate ways.

I am still financially conservative (or as my son would say, cheap), but I now like that fact about myself. I like the fact that budgeting expenses doesn't freak me out. Instead, it gives me a realistic picture of my financial situation and a sense of comfort knowing that my hard work has provided me and my family with a secure life.

I like that I have worked hard to achieve the professional success I enjoy and am proud of what I have created for myself. I have embraced the fact that I cannot change the reasons why I started working at such a young age or have methodically saved my money, but I like those aspects of my personality. Understanding why I started working so young and was hyper-focused for so many years is a great help as I examine what I want now in my life and make decisions about my future.

Had I not invested the time and effort to understand how I became who I am, and had I not sharpened my analytical and decision-making skills in the process, I would not be as effective as I am now at looking at what I want and figuring out how to proceed. Very likely I would have continued, disconnected, nose to the grindstone, clueless as to why I was doing what I was doing, and therefore lacking the impetus to change or the ability to enjoy the fruits of my efforts.

Using My Hypersensitivity to My Advantage

Another personal trait I developed from the rigors of my childhood that serves me well in the present is my ability to quickly read a room. Like many people who grew up with emotionally challenged parents, I have an uncanny knack to enter a room and, in a few brief moments, pick up on the emotional content of the people in it, whether it's a social or professional setting. I can intuit people's emotions like a built-in radar whether I'm in a boardroom, at a neighborhood barbeque, or at one of my son's tennis matches. It's not a skill I learned in college or law school, but that does not detract from its value to my success both personally and professionally.

Like Mad-Eye Moody from the Harry Potter universe, the key defining phrase of my childhood was "constant vigilance." I felt compelled to pay attention to what everyone in the house was doing, or more accurately, how everyone in the house was feeling.

In my mind, one wrong word or poorly timed question could set my mother off on a tirade about my personal failings and her deep disappointment or give my father ammunition to flippantly undercut my intelligence or goals and dreams. In my household, within a few moments of arriving home, I was able to ascertain the mood of each of my family members without a word being said.

Professionally, my ability to quickly understand emotional motivations or issues has been a core skill in developing my business and interacting with clients and prospective clients. However, it certainly wasn't always an asset in my personal relationships. As I grew up and left home, my ever-present "spidey sense" was often hypersensitive, which made me hyper-vigilant in personal relationships. Granted, this made me a fantastic boyfriend or friend at the start of a relationship, but the energy output needed to maintain that level of awareness drained me, and, worse, it often led me to change my behavior to please my new friends or girlfriends. Simply put, I was too attentive and consistently sold myself out in personal relationships for the fleeting moments of connection.

> *In my household, within a few moments of arriving home, I was able to ascertain the mood of each of my family members without a word being said.*

I needed and wanted connections so badly that I tried to be what the other person wanted and hid myself. So instead of seeking out people who genuinely liked me, I found whoever I could and tried to become what they wanted or what I thought they wanted.

This cycle would ultimately destroy most relationships because eventually the real me would want to come out, and I would be too ashamed to share my true self and instead would sabotage the relationship. Besides, I was too busy with all the emotional machinations in my head to be truly present in a relationship.

I did get lucky a few times and found a person who liked me for who I was, which made being me easier. Those happy accidents were few and far between, but the resulting friendships have lasted even as we fanned out across the country.

Over time and with intentional effort I was finally able to step back and understand how this superpower I had developed (hypersensitivity) was becoming an impediment for developing healthy, productive relationships, especially those that require some degree of intimacy. I was also able to accept my hypersensitivity as a valuable aspect of my personality and have learned how to redirect it to deepen relationships instead of undermining them.

How I effected this change in myself is the better story. First, I had to identify the trait or ability that was getting me into trouble. In this example, it was my hypersensitivity to other people's feelings. Next, I carefully examined my past to figure out where this trait or ability came from—and more importantly, why it developed. In this example I had developed it as a self-defense mechanism to avoid triggering negative reactions in my parents. Next, I examined how this trait or ability was being expressed or applied in my current life, and I increased my awareness of the harm it was causing to myself and others. Because I was no longer in the horror show of my childhood and was in a different world with different actors and circumstances, I did not need to be hypersensitive all the time.

> *I was able to accept my hypersensitivity as a valuable aspect of my personality and have learned how to redirect it to deepen relationships instead of undermining them.*

Once I was able to accept that I had this ability, borne out of my traumatic past, I looked for ways to use it more productively. For example, my hypersensitivity enables me to detect when one of the parties in a business deal is reluctant to express what is really important to them or what is keeping them from moving forward. My skill enables me to probe deeper to find out what that is, and then we can work on addressing it rather than flailing around and hoping to stumble upon a solution.

Now when I come home from work, if I sense something is off with Libby I do not immediately shift into either "how can I fix this?" or "what did I do?" mode, nor do I make a hasty retreat to the garage hoping she didn't notice I was home. Instead, I work to be honest and open and ask her how she is feeling. If she wants to engage with me (as she usually does), I listen attentively and with an open mind. I ask questions until I feel I fully understand, and only then are we prepared to move forward with a conversation nested in shared interests and compassion.

Accepting my "spidey sense" has been especially helpful in dealing with our son. I can tell when Nick is irritated or annoyed and when leaving him alone is the best approach or when he needs to talk but is reluctant to share. Sometimes he doesn't even realize it, but if I just sit with him awhile the words and feelings emerge. In those golden moments I feel great joy at the honest connection we have and thankful for the opportunity to engage with him in his introspective journey.

Simply changing how I applied my hypersensitivity completely transformed how I interact with people and has helped me create more meaningful and deeper personal and professional relationships.

Appreciating All of Myself

It has taken me a long time to accept that my rotten childhood could yield some positive character and personality traits and valuable life skills. Taking the good with the bad sounds so simple, but in practice it is a huge challenge. I can tell you from experience that trying to stuff down the pain, shame, and fear and erase memories of the past does more harm than good to yourself and others.

> **Pro Tip:** I strongly encourage you try to objectively examine your past in an attempt to create more positive associations in your mind; that is, to recall painful experiences and then find something good that came from each of them. This exercise gives you another superpower—the power to transform a negative into a positive.

Like most people I don't have total recall, but through thoughtful parsing and willingness to unpack my pain from the past, I have come to know myself and truly appreciate who I am (good and bad). I am thankful for my personal archeological dig because I discovered some great treasures. For example, one of the best memories I have is of a family trip to Rehoboth Beach, Delaware, when I was around ten years old, to visit my mother's family. I remember hanging out with my brother and sister, reading Archie comics, and my first crab bake. As I had done with my fond memories of playing baseball, I had glossed over those memories because of the painful experiences I had associated with my parents.

After I was able to piece together my personal history and

understand the value in it all, I realized I did not want to lose those memories. I still have all the bad ones, but I realized these good memories can coexist with the traumatic ones and that they add a depth and flavor to who I am.

I am the person I am today because I survived a very rough childhood—not the worst childhood, but I'm not looking for bragging rights. Take a look at your history with an objective eye. Try and identify all the good qualities and skills you developed as a result of your past. As I examined my past I began to realize that I needed to modify some behaviors that helped me survive in the past.

> *I still have all the bad memories, but I realized these good memories can coexist with the traumatic ones and that they add a depth and flavor to who I am.*

After we moved, I took that box of old trophies into the house and brought them out to show to my son. I had never talked with him about playing baseball and how much I loved it when I was a kid. I never told him about the laughing banter among my teammates or that the best part of those games was not winning or losing but being with friends and being myself. It was nice for me, and for him, to share these experiences together and for me to realize that I am who I am today because of it all.

All our experiences make us the people we are. It is up to us to accept their peaceful coexistence and learn to use them to fully become ourselves.

The takeaway is this: No matter how painful your past was, you survived it. You figured out a way through it. You have endured suffering and come out on the other side. You did it—nobody else did that or lived that life. You are stronger than you give yourself credit for. All the parts of your past contribute to who you are right now. Revel in joyful memories of the past and transform the negative into positive by identifying and redirecting the superpowers you developed during those difficult times. You can maximize their benefit to you in the present and continue to use them as you move forward.

Every part of your past contributes to who you are today. Embrace it all, accept yourself, and use the power of your past to shape a happier and more fulfilling future.

Now, an authentically happy family.
Libby, teenage Nicholas, and me, 2020.

Acknowledgments

There are many people I would like to thank for their help, guidance, and patience in the creation of this book. Considering the project took more than seven years, I am likely not remembering everyone who helped along the way, but I thank you all the same. I do hope that everyone who toiled in the ultimate creation is proud of the work.

Thank you, Libby, my wonderful wife and co-pilot on this fantastic journey. You inspire me and push me to get out of my head and experience my heart. Your compassion for others and thoughtfulness remind me of the good in people and how outreach and connection matter on a daily basis. Your patience and persistence in the drafting and editing process were integral to the book actually becoming a book.

Thank you, Mikal Belicove. You have worked with me for more than a decade on various projects as I worked to find a path to talk, share, and engage on what I have learned and experienced. We come from different worlds, and we have had to learn from each other how to coherently bring my thoughts to audiences.

I have learned much from you and cherish the process we have gone through together.

Thank you to the Amplify team led by Naren Aryal and Myles Schrag, as well as the marketing team—Nicole Sifers of Speakrbrand and Conner Krizancic of Good Wolf Marketing. You all had the task of teaching an old dog something new. You have been patient and instructive throughout this process. We are not here without your guidance and expertise.

Thank you, Mike Maroone, Ron Manwiller, Robert Omer, Sean Curley, and Shawn Turner. All of you read early versions of this book and provided candid and thoughtful feedback. For an insecure and fledgling writer, it was one of the scariest things to do, and each of you treated the request with grace and friendship.

Thank you, Lupe Samaniego—the best therapist for me. It seemed random to have met you, so bless the fates. You have always respected me, even as you learned of my shame and insecurities. With each discussion, you helped me understand myself and allow me (not someone else) to build the person I wanted to be. You are special.

Finally, thank you, Jason Wagner. Our friendship started when I needed it most (even though I did not know it at the time). For twenty-plus years, you have shown me tough love, tenderness, self-reflection, and genuine caring. Who would have thought a random class assignment in first-year torts would lead to this.

About the Author

Stephen J. Dietrich, JD, is a business attorney with over twenty-five years of experience in the private practice of law. He focuses on mergers and acquisitions, debt and equity financing, and restructuring transactions. He has handled and served as lead counsel on the purchase or sale of more than 300 retail vehicle dealerships, and he represents a variety of business entities and individual clients in day-to-day business matters. Among these are joint ventures, commercial real estate development, debt and equity finance, and corporate governance.

He received his JD from the Georgetown University Law Center, and his BA (summa cum laude) in political science from the University of Minnesota–Twin Cities. Stephen lives with his wife, Libby, and their son, Nicholas, outside of Denver, Colorado.

While Stephen's academic and professional background lies squarely in the world of law, he has long been on a personal mission to free others from the shackles of fear and anxiety that once prevented him from living a full, rewarding, and happy life.

Having endured his first eighteen years neglected by his mother and abused by his father, Stephen moved out and on to college, fully believing that he had left his past behind him.

He graduated college and then law school, landed a position at a reputable law firm, and got married. Little did he realize that the fear and resulting anxiety instilled in his youth had created deeply entrenched patterns of thought, emotion, and behavior that would continue to disrupt every aspect of his life.

As much as he wanted to eradicate the past from his memory, he came to realize that his past (both good and bad) held the keys to free him from the fear, anxiety, and disconnectedness that dictated his life. In this book, Stephen tells his story and hands you the keys to free yourself from whatever is holding you back from being your true, whole-hearted, and genuine self. These keys will help you live a rich, rewarding life governed not by anxiety and fear, but by facts, deliberation, emotion, and conscious mindful intent.

f @StephenDietrichJD   **in** /stephen-dietrich

O AuthorStephenDietrich

For more information
or to connect with Stephen, please visit:
StephenJDietrich.com